© Fernando Varanda, 1982

Printed and bound in Great Britain

Library of Congress catalog card number: 81-85164

ISBN 0-262-22025-3

# ART OF BUILDING IN YEMEN

# Fernando Varanda

Published with the assistance of The British Bank of the Middle East (A Member of
The Hongkong Bank Group) and the Aga Khan Program for Islamic Architecture
(Harvard University and the Massachusetts Institute of Technology).

Art and Archaeology Research Papers, London, England

The MIT Press, Cambridge, Massachusetts, London, England

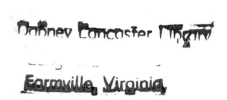
# FOREWORD

In this book I want to share something of what I have seen and admired in the art of building in Yemen. That art is to be found everywhere and in all types of building, from the simple reed huts along the Red Sea coast to the elaborate stone towers of the mountains, from irrigation channels and terraced fields to the formal design of a Sanʿaʾni house. To cover each aspect of such a rich and varied architectural tradition, however, would inevitably lose the sense of coherence of the whole. I have preferred therefore to capture that sense as best I can by associating and contrasting images in photographs and drawings, rather than by rigorous stylistic classification. And for the same reason the text has been kept to a minimum, in order to let the images speak for themselves. Only contextual reference has been made to 'monumental' architecture — both religious and secular — because I felt this was too wide and specialised a field to be encompassed by the present survey, and that it was not here that the originality of Yemeni architecture necessarily found its best expression.

This study contains some unavoidable, but still unfortunate, shortcomings: the information gathered could not always be checked; the transcription of names is not always accurate because of the difficulty in understanding local dialects; larger areas may be known by more than one name (I have generally chosen the more common designation); in some cases — Sanʿaʾ and the Tihama, for example — it has been necessary to condense a wealth of material that deserves a fuller discussion. For this I apologise. It should be stressed, moreover, that although I speak of Yemeni architecture, the documentation on which this book is based comes entirely from the Yemen Arab Republic. The wider area known as the Yemen (al-Yaman) is today divided between three states: the Yemen Arab Republic embraces the western and most of the northern portion (most of the mountain massif and the adjoining coastal strip along the Red Sea); the People's Democratic Republic of Yemen extends over the southern and eastern portion (Aden, the coastal zones on the Indian ocean, and the provinces inland, notably the Hadramawt);

the Kingdom of Saudi Arabia occupies the most northern portion (the oasis of Najran, the mountains of 'Asir and the adjoining coastal strip, which have long shared in Yemeni history and cultures. A study of the architecture of these neighbouring countries would provide a clearer picture of the mud architecture of the north and the stone and mud architecture of the south-east.

I had originally intended to record the processes of architectural change in urban forms after the Revolution of 1962 in the Yemen Arab Republic, but change is now so rapid that the information gathered is already out of date. Foreign aid pours in; major towns boom; new slums appear; the chief mason yields to the contractor; architecture and town planning become the subject of the office drawing board; the would-be house owner must now build clandestinely or subject himself to a complicated bureaucratic machinery. One hopes that the Yemen will resist the new and sometimes insidious cultural invasion and that the culture will assimilate the changes now taking place as well as it has done in the past.

This book is divided into two parts. Part One — Space and Form — presents the essentials of architecture in its natural setting, from agricultural terracing to houses and settlements. The introductory section is organised about a progression of forms, from the simple to the more complex. This progression is a formal and visual one and should not be understood as an argument about the historical evolution of settlement and architecture. In Part Two — Regional Surveys — areas of homogeneous construction are surveyed as far as possible in geographical sequence. These areas, homogeneous in terms of materials, building techniques and decorative styles, roughly coincide with the major natural regions and geological formations of the country. Although the areas in which different materials predominate can be defined (stone and mud in the mountains, reed and brick in the coastal strip), two or more materials are found combined in certain places, perhaps largely for reasons of status. In some regions of mixed construction one or another material dominates. When a mud top storey is built over a stone ground floor, the house style is determined by the stone work. However, when the stone section is built on a mud foundation, even up to a height of one or two floors, it is the mud section which determines the building style. Some combinations make a new synthesis in which neither material dominates.

The idea for this study started to take shape when in 1973 I took up a two-year assignment in the Yemen Arab Republic for the UNDP Town Planning Programme. At first I thought that my task was to supply the country with urban housing forms and techniques, but I soon learned that Yemen was already well endowed with both, and that it was more important to study how existing forms and techniques might best be developed to meet the needs of a country experiencing rapid change. In 1975 I returned to Sanᶜa' and began eight months of intensive travel and research into Yemen's existing architectural forms. Others supplied me with information and photographs about places which I could not visit and this helped me to form conclusions about what was general and what exceptional in this architectural tradition.

This study was made possible by the Calouste Gulbenkian Foundation, whose grant enabled me to do the necessary research and surveying between 1976 and 1978. I am also grateful to the Yemeni authorities — the Centre for Yemeni Studies, the Central Planning Organisation and the Ministry of Municipalities — who assisted me, as well as to the many local authorities and sheikhs who were so helpful.

The study incorporates the work of friends: Yemenis who received me, who travelled with me, who graciously opened the doors of their houses and did not make me feel an intruder with my peering lens and indiscreet survey kit; and Western friends in Yemen, and elsewhere, who generously gave me advice, information and encouragement. I would particularly like to mention Husayn Al-Quladhi, Husayn Makki, Husayn ᶜAlawi, Ahmad Al-Mansur, Abdul Aziz Al-Hajjar, Salah Aziz, Ali Hizan Al-Sabahi, Phyllis Crowell, Mark Calderbank, and Dr. Elliott Roberts who helped me in 1976 and provided a work base in the Research Centre of IPA. I am greatly indebted to Martha Mundy, who wrote the Introduction and whose careful checking of the typescript corrected many errors of transcription in the Arabic names; and to Dr. John and Sylvia Kennedy. Sylvia Kennedy is the source of many photos in this book. Other photographs were contributed by Kai Bird, Jerry Erbach, Gary Simantel, David Van Hammen, Dominique Hyance, Max and Suzanne Hirschi (who also supplied survey drawings). Marie Christine Fromont and Patrice Llavador contributed surveys, and Dr. Ronald Lewcock granted permission to reproduce drawings and photos from previous publications of his.

Special thanks are due to Etienne Renaud for the texts from which the sections on history and craft organisation are adapted: to Muhammad Massab, who spent much time travelling with me and compiled the introductory information on religious groups, tribes and social customs; to John Baldry for information on Tihama and Tihama towns; and to Anika Bornstein for information about the rural social organisation of Yemen.

Most of this study was completed in Lisbon at the Centre of Art and Visual Communication, whose director, Manuel Costa Cabral, I heartily thank. The maps and drawings were made from my survey sketches by Jaime Lebre with the collaboration of Ilda Fernandes and Frederico Mendes Paula; Jaime also designed the logos identifying the regional surveys. Thanks are due to Jorge Varanda for his renderings, and to José Octávio Fernandes, Manuel Silveira Ramos, Maria do Carmo, Galvao Telles and Charna Staten for their photographic work. I want to acknowledge the faith shown by the AARP team, my publishers, with special thanks to Jo Wodak whose sensitive editing made my text intelligible. Finally, thanks are due to The British Bank of the Middle East (A Member of The Hongkong Bank Group), whose generous funding made this publication possible.

# CONTENTS

# INTRODUCTION

*(Opposite) Top:* Sirwa town walls. *Centre Left:* Ma'rib dam wall. *Centre Right:* Map of pre-Islamic kingdoms. *Bottom Left:* Pre-Islamic lintel decoration incorporated into the door surrounds of the Sirha *(Yarim)* mosque entrance. *Bottom Right:* Ibex frieze on Ma'rib house wall, made partly of stones carved in pre-Islamic times.

Before proceeding to the sequence of photographs and drawings, some background to the history and culture of Yemen is necessary. This sketch should indicate the great antiquity of civilisation in Yemen and at the same time the wealth of political and cultural influence to which Yemen has been open over the course of history. The geographical position of Yemen at the south-west of the Arabian peninsula meant that it stood both on the periphery of the ancient centres of civilisation in the Fertile Crescent (which were subsequently often to be the political centres of Islamic empires) and at the entrance to the Red Sea where the sea routes met between Egypt, the Red Sea ports (notably, in the Islamic period, ports for the pilgrimage cities), East Africa and South Asia. Throughout history Yemen has been influenced by and contributed to developments in the northern lands of the Middle East, but by virtue of its relative isolation has retained a distinctive individuality, particularly in the mountain areas. Because of its strategic importance it has repeatedly been the object of attention by the empires of the time.

From the time of the earliest archaeological remains until the first century C.E. (Common Era) southern Arabian culture was centred in the kingdoms situated on the fringes of the eastern desert. Southern Arabian culture shared aspects of northern Babylonian and later cultures of the Fertile Crescent but had a marked individuality. The kingdoms depended upon control of the trade in frankincense and myrrh, which were produced on the southern coasts of Arabia and in Somalia and transported by caravans northwards to the cities of the Mediterranean and the Persian Gulf. One of the earliest of these kingdoms, and that which takes pride of place in the memories of Yemenis (as of Europeans in the legend of Sheba), was that of Saba' with its capital Ma'rib. Today the walled town of Sirwa and the ruins of the temple, elaborate dam and irrigation system in Ma'rib remain to bear testimony to the past of Saba'. Other kingdoms were Ma'in on the slopes of the *wadi* Jawf, Qataban, Awsan and Hadramawt.

In the first century C.E. these kingdoms began to decline as trade passed from the land route to sea routes through the Red Sea and the Persian Gulf. The centre of southern

Arabian culture and power moved to the Highlands — by the end of the first century C.E. the kingdom of Himyar had established its capital in Dhafar near the present-day town of Yarim. In the three centuries before the coming of Islam, Yemen witnessed great religious and political change, with the introduction of Judaism and Christianity and with the development of local monotheistic cults. In the 6th century C.E. Yemen was the object of Byzantine-Persian rivalry: an Abyssinian army invaded Yemen in defence of the sects of Christians supported by Byzantium; and in the last quarter of the century a Persian army supporting Judaism and Nestorian Christian sects was able to establish governors in many parts of Yemen. It was during this time that Yemen was converted to Islam. In the early Islamic period Yemen was divided into three administrative provinces: San'a', al-Janad near Ta'izz, and the Hadramawt.

Yemenis participated in the wars of conquest along with northern Arabs and they were to be active in the doctrinal developments of early Islam, notably in Shiism. The doctrinal movement which was to make the greatest mark in the political history of Yemen was that of Zaidism, one of the earliest forms of Shiism, introduced in Yemen towards the end of the 9th century C.E. by the Hasanite Yahya ibn al-Husain, known as al-Imam al-Hadi ila 'l-Haqq. Zaidism, while differing little in legal practice from Sunnite schools, advocated an active political role for the descendants of the Prophet in the person of the Imam whose duty is to establish a just government through applying his exemplary knowledge of Islamic law. The Zaidite Imams founded their religious centre in the northern town of Sa'da. In time the school was accepted by most of the population from Sa'dah to Ma'bar, but the coastal areas and the richer agricultural areas south of Dhamar were largely to follow the Shafi'i Sunni law school.

Although the Zaidis established themselves in the northern zones, most of the outstanding states in Yemen were to establish their capitals in the richer agricultural areas both of the coast, where spate-irrigation permitted intensive cultivation, and in the mountain areas of lower Yemen,

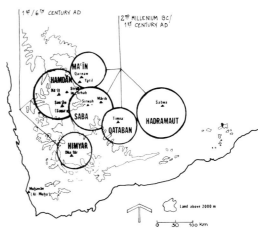

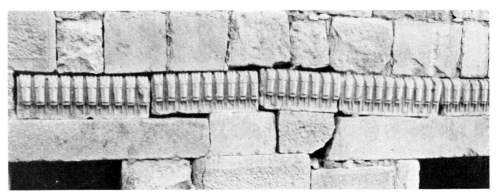

where extensive terracing captured the abundant summer rainfall. Thus, in the 11th century the Bani Najah made their capital in the splendid town of Zabid on the coast, in the 12th century the Sulayhid Queen Arwa founded her capital in Jibla in lower Yemen and in the 13th century the Rasulids established their capital in Taʿizz. The dynastic history of Islamic Yemen is very complex but can be reduced to a simple model. Time and again the central Islamic power of the day — the Abbasids, the Fatimids of Cairo, the Ayyubids — would appoint a governor, sometimes backed by military force, only for the governor or his descendants to start an independent dynasty with only formal links to the central power.

In the early 16th century C.E., spurred by the arrival of the Portuguese in the Red Sea, the Ottomans entered Yemen. They were to remain for a hundred years until they were ousted in 1639 by forces united against them under the Zaidite Imam al-Qasim. This period began to see the recension of the Zaidite Imams as a major political force in Yemen. A second Ottoman occupation of Yemen was later begun in 1860 in defence of the Red Sea and of the pilgrimage cities against European imperialism (1839 saw Aden declared a British protectorate and 1869 the opening of the Suez canal). Later, the Zaidite Imam Yahya Hamid al-Din united the northern tribes in opposition to the Turkish occupiers, and when at the end of the first World War the Turkish forces withdrew, he became ruler of what is today the Yemen Arab Republic. Although the Ottomans never controlled all of Yemen, they made an important contribution to the development of a central government in the form of the rudiments of central administration, a network of communications, and a series of fortresses at strategic points throughout the country.

The Imamic regime was based upon a union between administrators, who had religious status, and the military power of the northern tribal groups. The allegiance of these tribal groups was rewarded by selective alliances with prominent and wealthy sheikhs and was simultaneously controlled by a system of holding (and educating!) young hostages from the families of the major sheikhs. As the Imamic state developed an administration, it tended to institutionalise status differences. It entailed a duality between central and local legal institutions (those of Islamic law versus customary law) and between central versus local political authorities (the religious authorities versus the sheikhs). The tensions implicit in such duality have continued to mark recent Yemeni history. On the one hand, since the Yemen was essentially a self-sufficient agricultural economy, the government had to rely upon heavy taxation of the relatively productive Shafi'i farming areas, at the same time as it had to depend on the power of the northern sheikhs for the enforcement of its demands. On the other hand, the Imamic government sought to keep out foreign influence and economic change, fearing that this would result in demands for political change. But, although the Kingdom of the Yemen successfully resisted European colonialism, the Yemen could not remain isolated from changes in the world at large. Following the opening of the Suez canal, imports from Europe began to enter Yemen and to undercut local craft production: in 1949, following the assassination of Imam Yahya, the greater part of the Jewish community of Yemen, who as craftsmen had found times increasingly difficult, left Aden for the State of Israel. In 1962 the combined forces of young army officers trained in other Arab states and of various trading interests overthrew the Imamate. There followed a bitter seven-year civil war ending in 1969. In 1967 South Yemen saw the departure of the last of the British troops and the establishment of the People's Democratic Republic of Yemen. In 1969-70 the existence of the Yemen Arab Republic was secured in the north. Union of the two Yemens, although attempted on several occasions, has so far been prevented by ideological differences and by strong pressures from without. Today as yesterday the strategic position of the Yemen makes it the target of international competition.

The institutions of a modern centralised state are being developed — a modern army, a large bureaucracy, and an educational system strongly influenced by the Egyptians. At the same time the economy of the Yemen Arab Republic is becoming closely tied, through the mass migration of male labour, to the capitalist oil economies of the peninsula. Such radical changes have entailed the gradual demise of the status differences cultivated under the old regime, which marked the man of religious status and legal culture from the tribal arms-bearing farmer and from the man of the 'market'. The lowly status accorded to the craftsmen and service people of the marketplace, by the ethic of a traditional decentralised agrarian society, is today clearly something of the past. At present the agricultural sector is in gradual decline and the major sources of wealth lie abroad or in the cities. In spite of political pressures, the movement started under President al-Hamedi (d. 1977) towards national political integration remains a powerful force.

A new Yemen is emerging which seeks to rid itself of the worst of its past. May it also keep the best of its past.

# PART ONE: SPACE AND FORM

# 1. CONTROLLING THE ENVIRONMENT

The population of the Yemen Arab Republic of some 7 million is distributed over an area of 200,000 sq. km. that may be divided into five natural regions: Tihama, the Midlands, the Highlands, the Eastern Plateau and a portion of the desert known as al-Rubᶜ al-Khali.

The semi-desert coastal plain, Tihama, has a tropical climate and a population that is ethnically distinct, being predominantly African in origin. The Midlands have altitudes up to 1,000 m. split by deep gorges with streams running down to Tihama and to the Gulf of Aden. It is a fertile zone with a sub-tropical climate and heavy rains in spring and summer. The mountainous spine running from north to south constitutes the Highlands with altitudes over 3,000 m., a temperate and dry climate and rainy seasons similar to the Midlands but becoming less frequent in the north. The Eastern Plateau is semi-desert with mountains sloping down to the great Arabian desert, al-Rubᶜ al-Khali.

Prehistoric traditions and remains dating from the second millenium B.C. indicate that Yemen was one of the earliest areas to practice agriculture. The first agricultural settlements were probably along the fertile river beds (*wadis*) irrigated by flood water. As the population expanded, agriculture was extended up the mountain sides, and settlements moved from the *wadis* up onto the surrounding slopes. A well-balanced system of agriculture gradually evolved based on terracing and water conservation through an elaborate series of canals and masonry cisterns

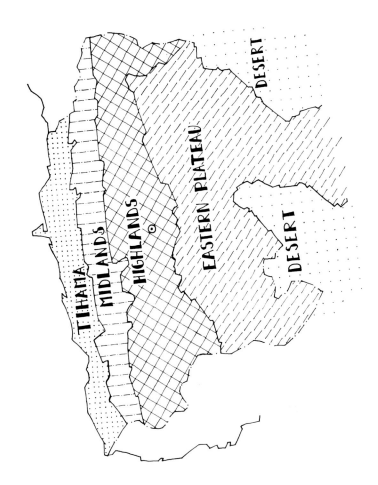

(*ma'jils*) which diverted run-off water to the terraced fields. Seasonal streams were controlled with cyclopean stone dams and flood breaks by a method that has since been forgotten. Only fragments of these pre-Islamic dams remain. Public and private wells complement the water supply, especially for domestic purposes.

The relationship between landscape and the built environment is most clearly demonstrated in the Midlands and the Highlands, and it is from these regions that most of the illustrations in the first part of the book are taken. *Top Right:* Schematic map of Yemen's five natural regions. *Above:* Northern Tihama.

*(Opposite)* Khubban in the central-eastern Highlands.

# 1. CONTROLLING THE ENVIRONMENT

*Above:* Hajja.

*Good morning, oh Naji, good morning friends and neighbours, tell me the story of the seeds, and what God wants with the sorghum. We have paid the zakat and made our prayers and see now the grace of God. We have charged the soil with fertilisers and see here the second harvest.* (Harvest Song, quoted in Bornstein)

*(Opposite) Top:* Haraz. *Bottom:* Masar.

The *ma'jil* is an open cistern that collects rain and run-off water. It takes various forms: round, rectangular, even an irregular, stone-lined hole in the ground. A standard *ma'jil* is composed of a large basin often linked by channels to one or two small basins where sediment is deposited. Animal troughs may adjoin the *ma'jil*, although this function may also be performed by the filtering basins. Ground water may be collected by holes slightly below ground level.

Pre-Islamic or Persian in origin, the construction of *ma'jils* has until recently been an important mountain tradition. Habur, for example, abounds in these and other sophisticated water works, though the skill has been lost and water is now mostly piped from artesian bores. *Left:* Shahara — terraces converging onto a *ma'jil*. Note the elaborate forms created by the steps leading to the basin. *Below:* Hajja *ma'jil* and steps descending to the lowest water level.

(Opposite) Top: Dharahan *ma'jil*. Bottom: Mahabisha *ma'jil*.

*Above and Left: Ma'jil* in al-Masu'd, said locally to be of pre-Islamic origin. The design is typical with a round central basin, small filter chambers and a simple stair to the lower levels. Local informants said that construction in rings had symbolic significance but could not explain it. Note the holes on the wall to collect run-off water.

*(Opposite) Top:* Detail of lime plastered wall in moat acting as a *ma'jil* for Bayt Na'ama in Bani Matar. *Centre Left:* Communal well, Dhamar. *Bottom Right:* Pre-Islamic dam of cyclopean stones near Sanaban.

# 1. CONTROLLING THE ENVIRONMENT

*Lock your door, protect your neighbour.* (Yemini proverb) One reason for property demarcation is to protect rights of access to water sources and areas irrigated mainly by run off water. Boundaries are usually defined by walls which may be little more than a line of piled rocks. *Below:* Boundary wall in Dharahan, punctuated by columns of loose stones serving as property markers or scarecrows. *Bottom:* Orchard wall on the periphery of Dhamar.

*(Opposite) Top:* Piled rock walls in Khamir.

Characteristic of mountain farmland is the guardhouse (*dayma*). It is especially common in the *qat* fields where night guards protect the valuable crop from thieves. Guardhouses show regional variations in form and material. They may be small mud or stone huts, perhaps of two storeys, with access to the roof by an external ladder. The more elaborate ones with an internal stair eventually evolve into tower structures, while retaining their surveillance function. These latter forms are closely related to the watch towers (*nawba*) that serve to protect an entire area that is frequently threatened by raiders. Watch towers may be isolated or in clusters detached from the settlement some distance away. They may eventually be absorbed into the settlement and transformed into dwellings, becoming an embryonic form of a house type characteristic of all the mountain areas. In Bani Ghurbayimi, for instance, the numerous cylindrical towers rise from the white rock bed of the barren fields some distance from the villages. In the southeast, an area subject to frequent raids, the desolate landscape is dotted with quadrangular tower dwellings. In times of peace, towers may be used as granaries and for storage.

*Centre:* Mud walls and tower guardhouses of vineyards at Khuraz near Saʿda.
*(Overleaf) Top:* Fields and stone guardhouses seen from Dharahan. *Below Left:* Two-storey mud guardhouse, Bani Hushaysh. *Below Right:* Tower guardhouse in al-Aʿsha, Saʿda region.

*Right:* Observation casement above watch tower door. *Below:* Section and plans of a tower occasionally inhabited. *Far Right, Centre and Bottom Left:* Watch towers in Bani Ghuthaymi. *Bottom Right:* Watch tower/dwelling in the south-east.

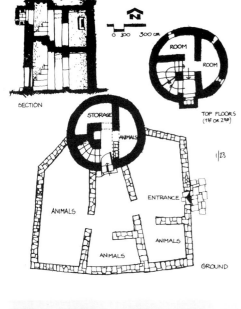

# 2. SHELTER AND SETTLEMENT

In Yemen the simplest form of shelter, made and carried by its user almost as an extension of his clothing, is the nomad tent found on the eastern slopes near the desert. Though grand tents can be found, the average bedouin tent reflects the frugality of nomad life. It may consist of a simple frame of stakes or branches over which carpets are thrown. Surrounding trees and shrubs supply additional 'furniture' — to hang gourds, more carpets, perhaps a crib — as well as shade. Sometimes only the women and children sleep within, the men sleeping on open ground.

Shelter is also provided by the many caves found throughout the country and used on occasion by nomads, shepherds and travellers. Lengthy stays in recent and in pre-Islamic times have usually resulted in elaborate adaptations. These caves also serve as places of refuge or hideout in times of war. Dharahan, for example, is built on top of a complex of caves with direct access to the sheikh's house. These are now used as stables, granaries and storage space; however in troubled times, the whole village may move into them. In the past permanent settlements may have occurred on some sites — in the Highlands, for instance, there are concentrations of natural, man-adapted and man-made caves called *himyari* by the local population, meaning 'before living memory' rather than definitely pre-Islamic, though many of these caves occur in sites rich in pre-Islamic remains.

*Top Right:* Door leading to Dharahan caves. *Centre Left:* Interior of *himyari* cave in Bayt Mahdan, Bani Matar. *Centre Right* and *Bottom:* Interior and exterior of garrison caves overlooking Thula, adapted by the soldiers who now live in them.

*(Opposite) Top:* Bedouin tent, Barat. *Bottom:* Caves in the mountainside at Shibam al-Qarhash, Bani Hushaysh.

## 2. SHELTER AND SETTLEMENT

*Saqif* (from *saqf,* roof) are stone constructions found throughout the mountains affording temporary shelter to farmers, shepherds and their animals. They have two forms: one roughly circular in plan, made of concentric rings of stone diminishing as they reach the top in a false dome; the other rectangular in plan, covered by stone slabs, supported by a series of parallel stone arches irregularly cut. *Top Right:* Shepherds in *saqif* near at-Tawila. *Centre Right:* Circular *saqif,* Haraz. *Bottom Right:* Rectangular *saqif,* Khamir. *Bottom Left:* Interior of rectangular *saqif,* Shahara.

*(Opposite)* The slopes of Hammam ᶜAli at the foot of Jabal Dawran are dotted with hundreds of *saqif*-type stone huts (2 x 3 m) and tents, seasonal accommodation for the many visitors who flock to the sulphurous springs and bath houses in January-February each year.

Rocky outcrops and ledges are frequently incorporated into built structures as though themselves suggesting the form that is constructed about them. It is not unusual to see such natural features integrating buildings in settlements which display a developed tradition of construction. However, it is in elementary communities that strong natural features more evidently suggest dwelling sites and basic house structures that man rudimentarily completes. *Left:* Al-Hada'. *Below:* At-Tawila.

*Right and Below:* Al-Juruf (the caves) of, Bayt Mahidin, Khubban. In this area there are several settlements where walls and roofs have been added to natural cave formations, thus adapting the caves for more or less permanent use. Al-Juruf has been inhabited for 13 generations and 15 families continue to live there despite the proximity of the main village. These particular dwellings were constructed during the Turkish occupation; tribal wars have led to similar settlements elsewhere.

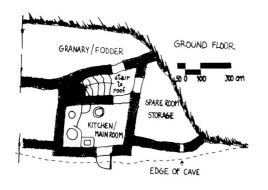

GRANARY/FODDER  GROUND FLOOR

stair to roof

SPARE ROOM STORAGE

50 0 100 300 CM

KITCHEN/ MAIN ROOM

EDGE OF CAVE

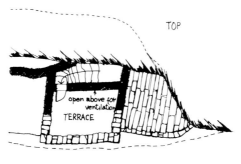

TOP

open above for ventilation

TERRACE

SECTION

## 2. SHELTER AND SETTLEMENT

On flat ground elementary settlements may still appear as topographical accidents — an extension of a terrace or an earth mound. These stone or mud huts occur in isolation or in beehive clusters wherein they often have interior connections. The construction and spatial organisation is simple, with a loose hierarchy of areas for living quarters, animal shelter and storage. There are usually no windows, the huts being lit and ventilated by top holes made by clay pots with broken bases which have been incorporated into the roof. Defence is an important concern; one explanation given for the houses being so camouflaged and without windows was the threat of Bedouin raids from the east. In larger settlements houses may be concentrated around a watch tower. *Below:* Hamdan.

*(Opposite) Top:* Rayda. *Bottom:* Near as-Suwaydiya.

## 2. SHELTER AND SETTLEMENT

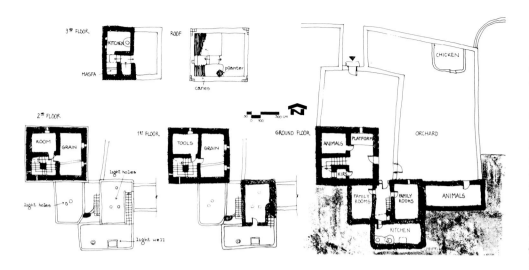

*Below:* Views of al-Khawa in the southeast. This is a more elaborate settlement with tower houses and low house structures on different levels with light wells. Bridges connect the roofs, which often contain plant boxes for aromatic herbs. Fire wood is commonly stored along the roof edges, giving these houses a peculiar aspect. *Left:* Plan of dwelling consisting of a small cluster of low houses and watch tower.

*(Opposite)* Plans, entrance, access to roof and interiors of low U-shaped houses in al-Khawa *(Top Right)* and as-Suwadiya *(Left and Bottom)*. The latter has two parts, a *funduq* (inn) with two rooms doubling as guest and store rooms, and a private area used by the family.

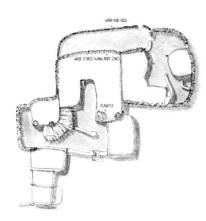

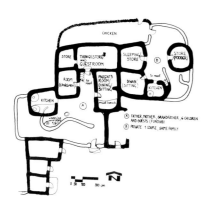

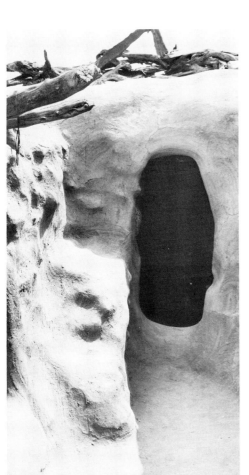

## 2. SHELTER AND SETTLEMENT

Al-Janad, the site of a famous early mosque, is composed of several clusters of houses, some connected from the inside. These houses are poor, the roofs being too fragile to walk on safely, the walls surfaced with mud, the floors dirt, and the branch structure of the ceilings exposed. The rooms are lit and ventilated by top holes. *Top, Centre and Bottom Right:* The main cluster and schematic plan of one section of the cluster. *Centre and Bottom Left:* The potter and his house.

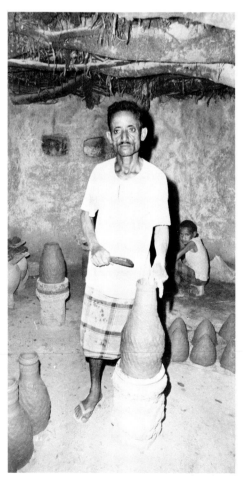

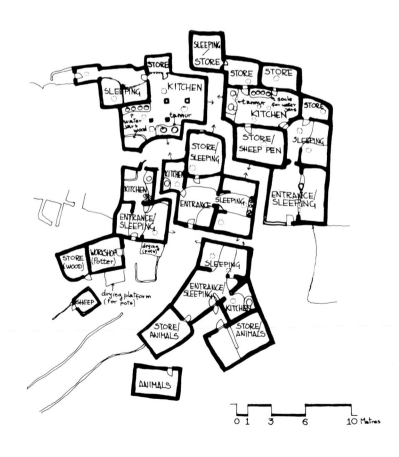

A homogeneous cluster of houses in al-Ajradi, in the south-east near the border with South Yemen. Set apart from other houses in the hamlet and perhaps part of the original settlement, these buildings represent a more developed house type with two storeys. The ground floor is reserved for storage, the kitchen and animals. The living quarters are on the upper floor, with access by an external stair. A more developed version of this house type occurs as the rural house in other areas of the country.

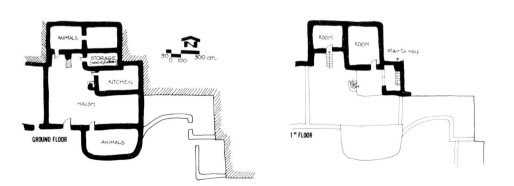

29

## 2. SHELTER AND SETTLEMENT

The process of settling probably started in the fertile *wadis*. As settlements grew they moved uphill, pressured by the need to save the best land for agriculture and by defence considerations. Added to the Yeminis' fondness of panoramic views, this has made mountain tops and hilltops the preferred locations for most Highland settlements. Villages blend so well with the surrounding landscape that, perched on the heights of a cliff, they are often hard to distinguish from the dramatic rock formations found in these parts.

In settlements on flat land or in valleys the lack of natural vantage grounds is compensated by watch towers that may constitute an advanced guardline. In other cases the defence requirements of a settlement or town are met by forts or citadels sited on high points overlooking the whole site. Most of these, found throughout the country, were built by the Turks.

The use of landscape as an immediate envelope for the house — and for passive defence — has so far been identified with settlements located in the most rugged areas of the country. The presence, in some, of towers punctuating the skyline suggests the existence of a different form of housing and way of defence - one that implies participation in war and the organisation of defence tactics.

*Below, in order from the Top:* The outskirts of al-Rhawda, Shamlan and Ghaw.

*(Opposite) Top:* Dhafar al-Ashraf. *Bottom:* Bani Murra.

*(Overleaf)* Al-Hajra, Haraz. The group of houses left of the main cluster was once used by the Jewish community.

## 2. SHELTER AND SETTLEMENT

The boundaries of most towns and villages in the mountains are defined by topographical features or by walls. In smaller hilltop settlements there may be an outer belt of houses with a blind wall facing away from the settlement continuing the rock formation. The ground and bottom floors of the dwellings, having no openings other than a few ventilation holes, constitute a hollow rampart unfit for habitation but adequate for stables and storage. The living quarters on the upper floors also provide good look-out positions. The remaining houses within the settlement may be low single- or double-storey types with an external stair. *Right:* Shooting holes in the stairway in a house of the Imam, Sanᶜa'. *Below:* Dhu 'Awlayin.

Freestanding outer walls are found in larger settlements on flat land or around mountain forts and citadels built for defence or as part of a larger military complex. Entrance is through a chamber with two gates opposite each other sometimes connected by a labyrinth. *Top Right:* Moat and village wall, Bayt Naᶜama, Bani Matar. *Top Centre:* Labyrinth gate, Thula. *Below and Bottom:* Bab Najran, Saᶜda.

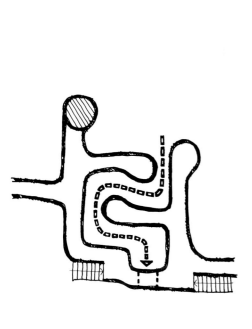

The size and complexity of a settlement reflects the composition of the group who inhabit it. Ideally, a hamlet is the home of members of the same family or lineage, a village that of members of the same tribe. Towns, by virtue of the heterogeneity of the groups who live there, tend to neutralise social differences. However, in the past, towns and big markets were often formally endowed with extra-tribal status; San'a', for instance, was under the protection of tribes adjoining the city.

*Bayt,* the word for 'house' which is used in Yemen to designate a patronymic lineage, may also be used for a 'small agglomeration' (an expanded farm complex, hamlet or village) often bearing the name of the original family who settled there. The house of the village leader is often the centre or starting point for the development of a *bayt.* His house may be the largest of a cluster; if it is of more recent construction outside the original nucleus it may also perform the role of a citadel in which members of the settlement seek refuge or protection. *Top Left:* Qa'bay, a typical isolated farmhouse in the mountains. *Bottom Left:* Sheikh's house in Qariya as-Sawda, with the mosque in the foreground. *Centre Right:* Sheikh's house and farm complex in at-Tir, A'zzan, overlooking a wide territory. Similar farming units in the surrounding low hills house the tribesmen of the sheikh.

*(Opposite)* Nua'ma, in the Hujjariya, is a small hilltop hamlet — a belt of houses around a rocky outcrop on which are built the chief's house, the mosque and the granaries. *Top Right:* Plans and section of chief's house. *Top Left:* Schematic plan and section of hamlet. *Bottom:* View towards the mosque.

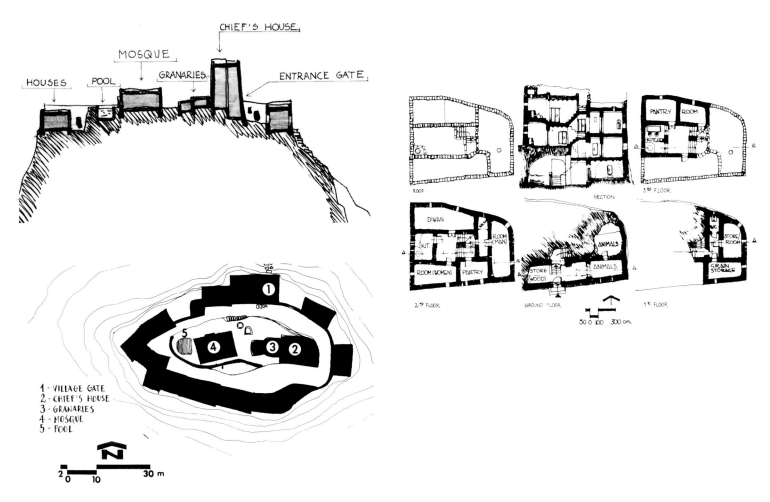

HOUSES   POOL   MOSQUE   CHIEF'S HOUSE   GRANARIES   ENTRANCE GATE

ROOF   SECTION   3ᴿᴰ FLOOR

DIVAN   ROOM (MAN)   KIT   ANIMALS   STORE ROOM   PANTRY   ROOM   KITCHEN

ROOM (WOMEN)   PANTRY   STORE (WOOD)   ANIMALS   GRAIN STORAGE

2ᴺᴰ FLOOR   GROUND FLOOR   1ˢᵗ FLOOR

50 0 100   300 cm

1 - VILLAGE GATE
2 - CHIEF'S HOUSE
3 - GRANARIES
4 - MOSQUE
5 - POOL

2 0   10   30 m

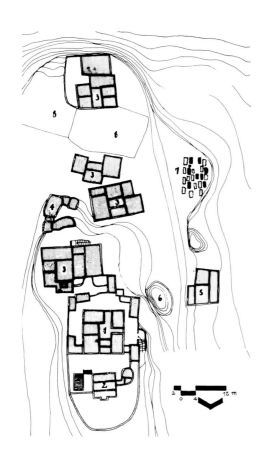

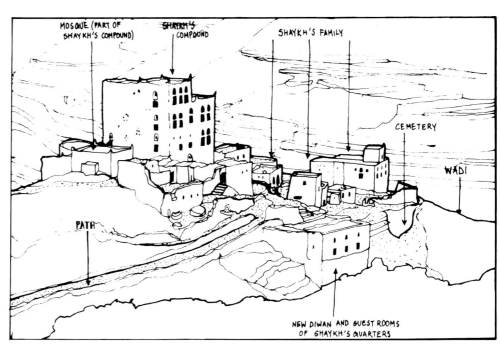

View (drawn from photo) and schematic plan of Bayt as-Sabahi. *Key:* 1. sheikh's house; 2. mosque (in sheikh's compound); 3. houses of sheikh's relatives; 4. 'poor man's' house; 5. new sheikh's *diwan*; 6. dung cake preparation pit; 7. cemetery; 8. threshing floors. *Below:* View from sheikh's house.

Bayt as-Sabahi is a small hamlet with six households belonging to the same family. It lies in a *wadi* amid cultivated fields. Originally this settlement was an outpost of the main clan stronghold on the hilltop guarding access rights to water against the rival clan group on the opposite side of the *wadi*. Later, part of the clan moved down from the hilltop, a reversal of the typical movement of settlements uphill away from the *wadi* to free fertile land for agriculture, and the present hamlet evolved.

The sheikh's house is the largest and highest, and also contains within its grounds the mosque and the main granaries, including the *madfan* (underground storage pits, protecting grain from theft, insects and humidity). Other communal facilities are outside the sheikh's house: the threshing grounds, combustible pits (depressions in the ground where dung fuel cakes are made) and cemetery. The houses of the sheikh and his relatives consist of two or more storeys, the ground floor being reserved for storage and animals, the upper floors being living quarters, one floor for each nuclear family unit.

Very different from the other structures is the 'poor man's' house, where an impoverished distant relation lives. This one-storey hut half-hidden between terraces, lit and ventilated by holes in the roof, is probably one of the earliest structures.

The detached new one-storey structure (more floors may later be added) consists of a small room, kitchen, toilet and *diwan*. The last is a large reception room in which tribesmen gather to discuss tribal matters, and where marriage and funeral ceremonies are performed. Originally a room in the sheikh's house was used for these purposes, but this special building was built when his house became too crowded.

*Top Right:* Plan of 'poor man's' house showing living quarters, kitchen, storage space and stables separated by walls leading to a central space like a primitive court open from one side. *Centre and Bottom Right:* Ground floor plan and section of sheikh's house. *Mid-and Bottom Left:* Sleeping/reception-room and kitchen of sheikh's house.

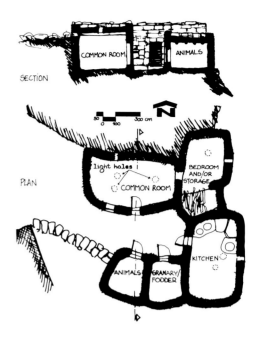

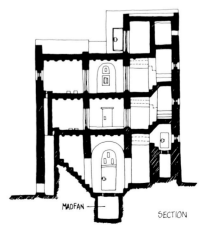

## 2. SHELTER AND SETTLEMENT

Mithal is a small village in the region of al-Hada', where the central Highlands of settled farmers join the eastern slopes touching the great Arabian desert — a land of fierce warriors known for their cunning and rapacity, where bedouin raids, tribal wars and blood feuds are part of living memory. The village is situated in a landscape of rolling hills with higher mountains beyond. On one small elevation lies the village proper; on another next to it is the present sheikh's house; on another more distant hill is the former sheikh's house (father of the present sheikh). Between these two houses lies a group of low constructions sheltering granaries, warehouses and stables, and a small house which was once the present sheikh's and is now used by occasional travellers, shepherds, nomads, etc. Shown diagrammatically *(below)* the houses of the present and former sheikhs have positions of strategic logic: the former sheikh's house is like an observation outpost and the present sheikh's house is like a citadel or castle for the village nucleus.

The present sheikh's house (see p. 194) consists of three houses, built at different times and joined together so that a line of outer rooms protects an inner core lit through light wells. In times of war, the community seeks refuge and defence is organised here.

In the village itself live close relatives of the sheikh (in the larger houses), other tribesmen and other occupational groups called *bayya*[c] (those who sell) like the butcher, weaver, potter, barber, bath attendant, and so on. The plan of the village is closed, the houses making an outer belt of blank wall with a single entrance gate. Outside the main settlement is the mosque (between the village and the present sheikh's house) and a couple of shops (in front of the gate) supplied regularly by cars from the main centres. The population still goes to the *suq* of the area. *Below:* Mithal village and the sheikh's house.

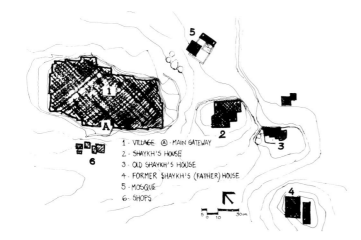

1 - VILLAGE  Ⓐ - MAIN GATEWAY
2 - SHAYKH'S HOUSE
3 - OLD SHAYKH'S HOUSE
4 - FORMER SHAYKH'S (FATHER) HOUSE
5 - MOSQUE
6 - SHOPS

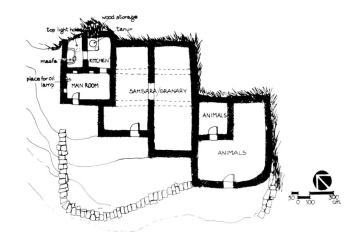

*Top Right and Left:* Plan and interior of the present sheikh's previous house partly built into a small mound. The stone walls are coated with mud. Pegs protruding from the walls are used to hang clothes, guns and so on. The living quarters are less important than the space allotted for storage and animals. Adjacent is the sheikh's combustible pit. *Centre:* Similar village houses.

## 2. SHELTER AND SETTLEMENT

Many settlements have communal agricultural facilities: threshing floors, places for the preparation of dung fuel, animal enclosures or stables, storage places for fodder and, sometimes, granaries (not in the case of tower-houses). In smaller villages, the sheikh may store in his house the grain supply of the whole village. *Top Right:* Threshing sorghum in Taᶜla, Suhar. Harvested grain is brought to a communal threshing floor (*al-jurn*) and, when dry, threshed with a stick. Barley and wheat may be ground by means of a large stone dragged over the grains by oxen or donkeys. *Centre Right:* Threshing floor, with grain drying on roof tops in the foreground, Bani Qaysh. *Centre Left:* Animal fodder stacked in a tree, Wadi Bana. Each family in this region has its own tree for this purpose. *Bottom:* Hay-stacks in Dharahan. In the foreground is the entrance to the communal storage and animal pens in the caves beneath the village.

*Top:* Stable and pits for making dung fuel in al-Hanaka, Radaᶜ. Because wood is scarce, animal dung is shaped into flat discs and sun-dried to make a slow burning fuel with high caloric power. *Centre:* Animal pens off the main thoroughfare through al-Kitba, Khubban. Such enclosures in the streets are common. *Bottom:* Communal oil press in al-Mawra, Khubban, comprising a stone vase and grinding stones activated by the circular path of a blindfolded camel. In front a cow is hand-fed dry fodder wrapped in green leaves. To the left is the door of a small general store which functions also as the local tea house and meeting place for the village.

## 2. SHELTER AND SETTLEMENT

Access to mountain villages is difficult and most can be reached only by foot, donkey or at best four-wheel-drive vehicles. However, traditional roadways exist: paths and steps carved into the mountainside, bridges over vertiginous chasms. Some of the road network built by the Turks remains. *Top:* Donkey riders en route to al-Rawda. *Below:* Bridge connecting the main part of Shahara with a subsidiary settlement.

At intervals along these paths drinking wells or covered fountains (also found in markets) have been built on the initiative of mosques or local landowners to fulfil the pious duty of giving water to the thirsty. *Centre Left:* Paved section of the Turkish military road network still in use at Qariya al-Sawda, Radaᶜ. *Centre Right:* Steps leading from Thula to the fort above. *Bottom, Left to Right:* Fountain carved in the rock wall at one entrance to Manakha; fountain in the market place at Khamir; fountain on the road to al-Zaraja, al-Hada'.

*(Overleaf) Top:* Carrying water, Haraz. *Bottom:* Water duct leading from hilltop reservoir to great mosque in Dhi ᶜAshra, Khubban.

Water for domestic use is generally transported by donkeys or hand-carried by women. Larger settlements may have masonry water conduits leading from a distant point of collection to a distribution point near or inside the town. The pre-Islamic method of bringing water from hilltop reservoirs through a series of intermediate basins and locks to distribution points for domestic or agricultural use still operates in some places. *Left:* Pipes laid directly on the ground near al-Sumaᶜa. *Below:* Water conduit, part of the old system, and new pipe *(foreground)*, in Ibb.

According to the Koran, water is the beginning of all life. A place of water — stream, pond or *ma'jil* — may become a place of prayer, ablutions being a fundamental part of Islamic ritual. Most mosques are endowed with an ablution pool *(sabil)* which may also supply part or all of the community's water requirements, functioning in the same way as a *ma'jil*. *Top:* Friday at the waterfall and pool in al-Mawra, Khubban. Men make their ablutions and prayers on top of the ledge while children play in the pool. *Centre Left:* A swimming lesson in the *sabil* at Jibla. *Centre Right:* A man having his hair shaved before prayer at al-Mawra pool.

*Centre Left and Right:* This *ma'jil,* on the outskirts of Dhamar, has a paved area containing a stone inscribed with the name of Allah indicating the direction of Mecca. This provides a prayer ground for anyone who wishes to make their ritual ablutions. Thus, a water place can become a sacred place for prayer. *Bottom:* A small mosque and adjacent pool at Kuhlan. The size of this large pool signifies its importance as a water supply for the community, rather than just for the mosque.

The *sabil* of Dhi Bin's mosque and *madrasa*.

## 2. SHELTER AND SETTLEMENT

Annexed to the *sabil* in the larger mosques are bath houses where ablutions may be performed in private. These are rows of small quadrangular rooms, roofed by domes, with a small pool usually connected to the *sabil* by holes or conduits. *Centre Left:* Bath compartments surround the *sabil* at Saᶜda. Only the corner bath houses are domed. *Centre Right: Sabil* and bath houses of the Great Mosque at Jibla. *Bottom Left, Right and Above:* Foot stones in the ablution area and bath house domes of the al-Mukhtaribiya Mosque, Taᶜizz. *Top Right:* Plan and section of hot water bath houses in Hamman ᶜAli, showing the inflow, overflow and waste-water systems.

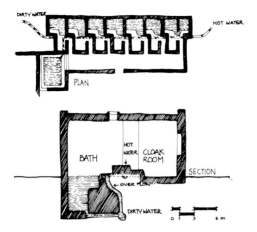

A refinement of the bath services traditionally provided by the mosque is the public bath *(hammam)*. These are found only in the largest cities (Sanᶜa' has 18) and are run by hereditary bathkeepers who charge a small fee. A typical *hammam* consists of a group of small rooms graded in temperature from cold through temperate to hot. Water is piped from the well and reservoirs in the yard, through a hot boiler or cold pond next to the bath. The floors in the hot rooms are heated by hypocausts and the walls by vertical flues, about two-thirds of each bath being subterranean, thus conserving heat. The fuel consists of skin and bone refuse from the slaughter yards and dried human excrement. The ash that remains after burning is sold as fertiliser for vegetable gardens and orchards. *Top:* Dressing room of Hammam al-Shukr, Sanᶜa'. *Bottom:* Domes of *hammam* in Yarim. Note the small skylights.

## 2. SHELTER AND SETTLEMENT

Mosques are associated with even the smallest settlements and are often located outside settlements in order to serve travellers as well as local inhabitants. A complete mosque has a prayer hall with *mihrab*, courtyard, ablution pool, bath houses and a minaret. Small mosques may lack some of these features, while large ones may have more than one *mihrab* and minaret, a central court with the main prayer hall on the side facing towards Mecca and open colonnades on the other sides. Larger towns have at least one great mosque — the *jamic* — a congregational place of assembly for the community at Friday noon prayer. Until the appearance of the radio a generation ago it was, like the market, a centre for the exchange of news. It is also a place for rest and study, administering education to all levels until the recent creation of secular schools.

The most common mosque type has a rectangular plan with a flat roof supported by wood beams, columns and arches. The oldest mosques in the Highlands (al-Janad, the Great Mosque of San'a', etc.) and most mosques in small towns are of this type. Domed mosques generally reflect foreign influence introduced by the ruling classes, either in workmanship or design, and, in the Highlands, a monumental intention. In the south and in Tihama most mosques, even small ones, are domed, probably as a result of Indian craftsmanship.

Decorative treatment in mosques is usually subdued though there are some remarkable carved and painted wooden ceilings and wall paintings. The stone, brick and plaster decoration of domes, *mihrabs* and arched doorways displays ornamental themes and techniques related to the secular architectural tradition.

*Centre Left:* Manakha. *Centre Right:* Qariyat al-Sawda, Radaᶜa. *Bottom:* Al-Magraba.

*(Opposite)* The village mosque of Mithal contains a prayer hall, courtyard, pool and bath houses. The raised stones in the corners, said to be dedications to Islam (called *shahada*), are characteristic of all flat roofed mosques and many houses. Tradition has it that the builder puts as many stones in each corner as the number of people assisting him at the time.

*Right:* Prayer hall and courtyard, Qariyat al-Sawda, Rada⁣ᶜ. *Below:* Central court and prayer hall of Great Mosque, az-Zaydiya, Tihama.

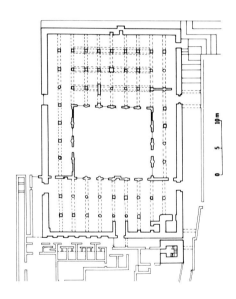

Prayer hall, courtyard and plan of Great Mosque, Shibam al-Aqyan.

57

# 2. SHELTER AND SETTLEMENT

*Right and below:* Minaret and prayer hall of Great Mosque, Harib.
*(Opposite)* Prayer hall of Great Mosque, Zabid.

*Left:* Mosque al-Bakiliyia, San⸢a'.
*Below:* Mosque al-Mukhtaribiya, Ta⸢izz.
*(Opposite) Top:* Mosque in Hays.
*Centre:* Mosque in al-Mansuriya. *Bottom:* Mosque in Bayt al-Faqih.

Though the call to prayer was originally made from the mosque roof (minarets being prohibited by the early Zaydi Imams), minarets were later added to existing mosques. The minaret, the place for the prayer call, is also an emblem: the more important a mosque, the higher and more decorated its minaret, at times being the only striking feature of an otherwise dull exterior. Minarets are usually of brick even when the mosque itself is of stone. Today loudspeakers are often added. *Left:* The twin minarets of Mosque al-Ashrafiyyah, Taᶜizz. *Bottom Left:* Unusual stone minaret in Sadda. This one is particularly remarkable in the way it translates into stone the filigree quality of brick minarets. Loudspeakers can be seen on the top. *Bottom Right:* A new mosque in Dhamar.

*(Opposite) Top:* Sanᶜa', a city of 64 minarets. *Bottom Left to Right:* Minaret of the Great Mosque, al-Rawda; minaret of Dhafar al-Ashraf mosque; small minaret in the congregational mosque of Dawran.

## 2. SHELTER AND SETTLEMENT

Rural markets function as local trading posts for basic goods and as a distribution system for surplus and imported commodities. The market may consist of open spaces where tents and awnings can be set up, or of rudimentary permanent stalls of mud or stone. A small community — a family of caretakers, perhaps — is usually attached to the market place, though this community has no tribal rights and lives under the protection of the local sheikh. Markets are held within towns or in special areas several miles away where they are used by all the surrounding villages. Thus a town of some size and importance may have only a small subsistence market or no market at all, while a few miles away an important market is held each week. Permanent daily markets in large urban areas are usually found in the immediate vicinity of the great mosque or pilgrimage mosque. Such markets have a particular spatial organisation; trades and crafts, each having its own headman, are located in specific areas or streets. A chief is elected from the headmen to decide on general regulations, prices, etc. Common in urban markets is the *samsarah* (warehouse), where caravans unload and merchandise is stored. The *samsarah* can double as an inn, the upper floors providing accommodation for merchants. Many of the *samsarahs* in the major centres are now abandoned as caravans are replaced by cars and lorries. Teahouses and restaurants provide places to meet and rest. Sparsely furnished, their decoration consists of covering the walls with colourful patterned fabric, and, more recently, enamel-painted animal and plant motifs. *Bottom Left:* Open market in the streets of al-Bayda'. *Bottom Right:* Market day, Taᶜla, Sahar.

*(Opposite) Top:* Taᶜla, Sahar. *Bottom:* Valley market, Qa'bay.

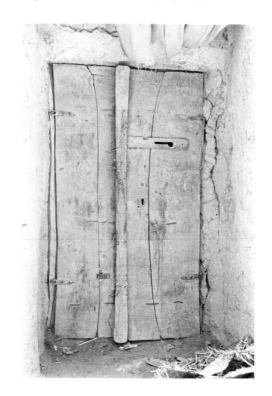

*Top:* Stalls of weekly market at Buaᶜan, Bani Matar. Merchandise is now sold closer to the busy tarmac road *(left)* leaving most of the old stalls empty. *Bottom Left:* Market street, Manakha. *Bottom Right:* Door of market stall, Huth.

*Top:* Market stalls in Saᶜda in front of the Great Mosque. *Centre:* Market and Great Mosque, at-Tawila. The urban market and congressional mosque, side by side, usually define the communal centre.

## 2. SHELTER AND SETTLEMENT

*Right:* Section and ground floor plan of Samsarah al-Majjah in San'a'. *Centre Left: Samsarah* in al-Mahwait consists of a porticoed gallery with stores and an upper floor with stores and lodgings opening onto a wide courtyard. *Bottom:* Samsarah al-Waqf, Sa'da.

*(Opposite) Top Right:* Tea house and inn in Suq al-Milh, San'a'. *Top Left:* Teahouse in the main market square, Sa'da. *Bottom:* A rudimentary teahouse/restaurant in al-A'sha on the road to Sa'da.

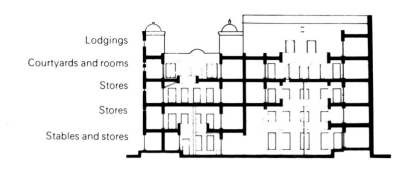

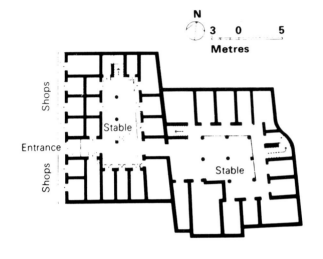

## 2. SHELTER AND SETTLEMENT

The sheikh, the traditional rural leader, may be the head of a small settlement or the leader of a vast confederation of tribes. The sheikh collects the tax prescribed by the Koran (the *zakat*) and maintains tribal law, thus assuming a function like the *qadi*, the religious judge. In most parts of the country there is a central government representative, the *'amil*, whose role is to maintain law and order and to implement governmental policies, and a centrally appointed religious judge or *hakim*. The higher levels of the central administration have their seats in the major cities.

Buildings which house these representatives of power are only distinguished by their size and refined detail. Otherwise the local sheikh's house is similar to others in the same village. The houses of leaders who command a larger community are usually more elaborate, being equipped to receive large gatherings and able to function as a fortress if necessary. In major centres citadels and forts are the special preserve of the military, and the quarters of the former Imamic rulers or the nobility are sometimes taken over for specific administrative functions. These

buildings, reflecting the taste of their previous occupants, often introduce styles prevailing in the cities to provincial areas. *Top:* The Hukuma (government centre) of Dhamar — a mixture of local and San<sup>c</sup>a' styles. San<sup>c</sup>a' influence is visible in the brick construction friezes and windows while local traditions contribute the mural plaster decoration with free rendering of stylised ibexes and lilies. These themes are pre-Islamic in origin, the lily being probably a stylisation of a bull's head. *Centre:* Fort outside al-Dahi, Northern Tihama. In an area where the domes-

tic architecture is almost all reed, except for the few houses of the town notables, this structure was built by the Turks in brick as part of their network of forts along the coastal strip.

The following pages present typical urban networks and street spaces. The location of houses and the quality of their architectural finish indicate social status. Socially segregated groups (like the Jews in certain areas) were sometimes spatially separated as well: outside town walls or adjoining a settlement at one end. Slums and sub-standard housing appeared only after the Civil War, with the boom in the major urban centres. The urban drift is indicated by these figures (taken from the Central Planning Organisation Yearbook for 1975): *'There are eight major towns in Yemen (larger than 25,000 people) with 8 per cent of the total population. Smaller towns (5,000-20,000) account for another 15 per cent. In 1970, 80 per cent of the population were farmers. In 1980 this population is estimated as 60 per cent (for 40 per cent urban dwellers).'*

*Above:* Thula, city of tall stone buildings, seen from the fortressed hill overlooking it. The great mosque *(foreground)* adjoins the market; away from the city centre and near the walls is the *hukuma (upper left)*, a large brick building in Sanᶜa' style.

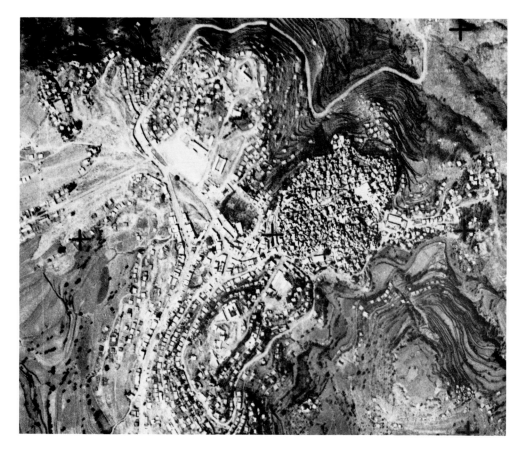

*Top:* Ibb, the main city of one of Yemen's most fertile areas. The city's older nucleus, and still its main core, is located on the highest of several hills at the foot of a mountain. After the end of the Civil War and with the opening of a new asphalt road connecting two of Yemen's largest cities — San<sup>c</sup>a' and Ta<sup>c</sup>izz — the city has expanded beyond its former walls and natural boundaries and progressively occupied first the valley, where the road goes and where a new government-built market is located, and then the nearby hills and cultivated land.

*Bottom:* Sa<sup>c</sup>da in 1969. The centre of Zaydism, the religious sect followed by most Highlanders, the city is situated in the middle of the semi-desert northern plains. The striking contrast between urban space contained inside the walls and the emptiness outside is no longer found today. New construction follows the new road to San<sup>c</sup>a' leading out of Bab al-Yaman *(on the right),* the main southern gate the labyrinth entrance of which was destroyed to give access to car traffic. The second main gate, Bab Najran *(on the left),* was preserved with its labyrinth intact until recently. On top of a small elevation in the line connecting the two gates is *al-qahira,* the fort, now the headquarters of the military garrison. The Great Mosque *(below right)* adjoins the market square where administration buildings are located. The large empty spaces *(lower part)* are sunken orchards. As in San<sup>c</sup>a', these are lower than ground level, apparently because they have been planted in areas excavated to provide mud for building.

Dhamar, an open city, is the only town of considerable size without walls or any natural protective boundary. It is set in the middle of a vast plain, guarded by a couple of small villages on nearby hills which define a defensive perimeter (the two closest ones being called the 'Horns of Dhamar' and 'Tail of Dhamar'). The city is ancient, supposedly founded by Dhamar 'Ali, a *himyari* king who restored the dam of Ma'rib, and has been known in the more recent past for its Koranic university and its horses. It is also the main trading centre for a large number of tribes in the neighbouring provinces. The market *(visible in the middle of the picture)* is like a miniature replica of the city itself with its paved streets and urban layout. It is also a meeting place for the socially and tribally varied neighbourhoods which are organised in relatively autonomous clusters (the most dramatically isolated being the old Jewish quarter, 'closed in' with access gates). The Great Mosque is some distance from the *suq,* next to which is a congregational pilgrimage mosque. Commercial buildings and houses are being constructed along the new asphalt road to San<sup>c</sup>a' *(on the left),* and a new central market west of this was under study.

## 2. SHELTER AND SETTLEMENT

The character of a settlement is revealed in its street spaces. Thoroughfares between houses are often a no-man's-land where waste is thrown, but they are enriched by the main, and often elaborate, facades of the houses which always face the street. Streets are also spaces where children play and marriage dances and processions take place. In larger towns, small neighbourhood streets serve as gathering places for women who come out to take fresh air just before sunset, chat with their neighbours and watch over the play of small children. Although stone-paved streets are still seen in some towns, there are few remains of traditional paving. *Top Left:* Stone-paved steps leading from the main gate, Ibb. *Top Right:* Wall textures in the narrow streets of Barat. *Below:* Men dancing before a marriage celebration, at-Tawila.

*(Opposite)* Manakha.

## 2. SHELTER AND SETTLEMENT

Modern plumbing has produced some curious results. This recently introduced trade is often hastily acquired and a plumber may think nothing of taking a pipe down the middle of a wall and across a window. No doubt the unusual effect of this street 'furnishing' will be lost as this trade comes under greater control. *Centre, Left and Right:* Ibb. *Bottom, Left and Right:* Sanᶜa'.

# 3. THE HOUSE

*'A man in his house is worth so much that even when he's dead it takes four men to carry him out.'* (The Marquis of Pombal)

A man's house is his castle: the Yemeni's pride in his house is reflected in its spatial organisation and in its appearance which is important in shaping the environment. In terms of spatial organisation there are seven main house types in Yemen: four in the mountains and three on the coastal plain (the latter three are described in the regional surveys presented in Chapter Five). In this chapter, examples of house types already illustrated are reviewed, in particular the tower house whose spatial organisation contains all the elements observed in other types. *Right:* Schematic house-type distribution in the mountains.

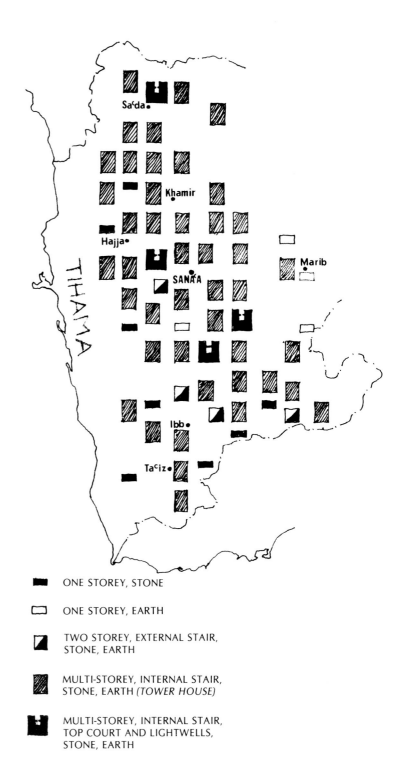

■ ONE STOREY, STONE

▭ ONE STOREY, EARTH

◪ TWO STOREY, EXTERNAL STAIR, STONE, EARTH

▨ MULTI-STOREY, INTERNAL STAIR, STONE, EARTH *(TOWER HOUSE)*

⬛ MULTI-STOREY, INTERNAL STAIR, TOP COURT AND LIGHTWELLS, STONE, EARTH

# 3. THE HOUSE

The most elementary house has one storey and is built in stone or stone and mud. Divided into rooms for living, animals and farm storage, the shape of this house is adapted to natural features of the landscape or to other houses of the same type, forming clusters. The house often has no windows, being lit and ventilated by holes in the roof, and there is no sanitation. The plain interior surfaces are treated with mud. On the fringes of the Eastern Plateau, the one-storey houses, made of mud, have detached quadrangular plans with the same internal organisation, small square windows and sometimes an interior stair indicating a possible extension in height. Bands of red ochre decorate the top and bottom of the walls and frame windows and doors. *Below Left:* Roof of one-storey stone house in al-Qifla built against a slope which forms its back wall. Notice the roof holes. *Centre Right:* One-storey house in Maᶜbar with a stair to the roof signifying that an upper floor may be added later. *Bottom, Left and Right:* Schematic section, plan and interior of a *funduq* in al-Qifla. The interior, marked dining/ bedroom on the plan, is lit by roof holes and is also the family dressing room. The family rooms (see plan) are only used when the main house is full of guests, otherwise they are for storage.

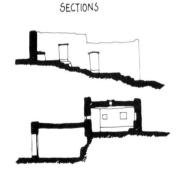

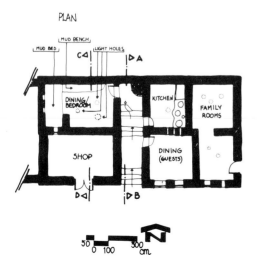

A second house type, built in stone, mud blocks, or stone and mud, has two storeys with an external stair to the living quarters on the upper floor. The ground level is used for storage and animals and sometimes contains the kitchen. Sanitation is generally not included. The windows consist of regular opening shutters with a separate fanlight above. Interiors may be finished with lime or gypsum plaster, but are more usually surfaced with mud. Parapets and windows may be adorned with simple decorative motifs. This house type usually occurs in rows and is common in the small settlements transitional between Midlands and Highlands. *Top and Centre Left and Centre Right:* Exterior, living room and survey of a simple form of two-storey house, Rubat al-Qa'lah, Yarim. The living room is plastered, with a mud skirting. *Bottom Left:* House in Sirha, Irian. The living rooms lead to a semi-covered hall or court. *Bottom Right:* House in Bayt Na'ama, Bani Matar. Note the small living quarters compared to the ground floor service areas.

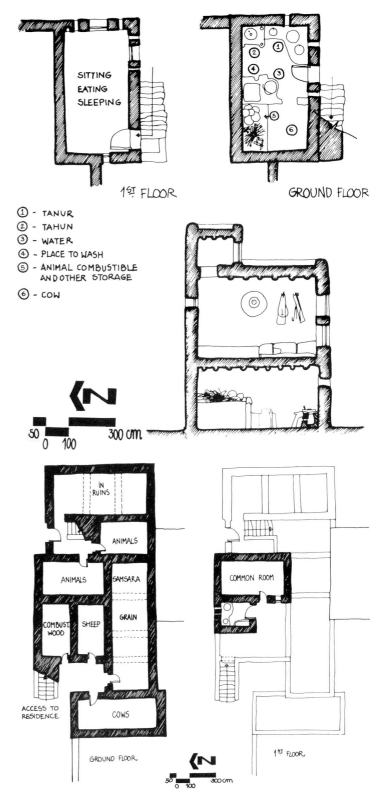

1ST FLOOR     GROUND FLOOR

① - TANUR
② - TAHUN
③ - WATER
④ - PLACE TO WASH
⑤ - ANIMAL COMBUSTIBLE AND OTHER STORAGE
⑥ - COW

50  100  300 cm
0

ACCESS TO RESIDENCE

GROUND FLOOR     1ST FLOOR

50  100  300 cm
0

## 3. THE HOUSE

The tower hosue, derived from the watch tower, is built of earth, stone, baked brick, or combinations of these materials, with two or more storeys and interior stairs that allow vertical expansion as more space is needed. A common feature is the *shubaq,* the observation casement, also used for a cooling water box though, in the watch tower, it has a solely strategic function. Though circular forms are found, the quadrangular plan is most common. Light and ventilation are usually provided through windows and wall ventilation slits *(shaqus),* though additional light may be provided by fanlights of alabaster or coloured glass set in stucco tracery frames which cast richly coloured patterns. These houses make full use of the decorative possibilities of structural materials (with friezes and decoration of openings) and the interior surfaces in plaster may be elaborately carved. Bathroom and toilet facilities are included within the house.

*Top Right:* House of a wealthy family in San𝑐a' designed to display the taste and affluence of its owners. *Top Centre:* Section showing schematic spatial organisation. *Bottom Right:* Isolated farmhouse in 𝑐Abbas, a desolate sparsely populated region in the south-east where defence is of paramount importance. *Bottom Left:* Round tower house in Shamlan with additional quadrangular rooms on top, a frequent form in the San𝑐a' region. Function is also indicated by the construction material; mud for the lower storage levels, brick for the upper living quarters.

*(Opposite) Top Right:* Low house with tower, al-𝑐Uqla. Such compounds are common in isolated farmhouses, when the tower is used both for storage and defence. *Bottom:* Round tower houses, Wadi Dahr, built as dwellings (watch towers are built in the cliffs behind). Note the *ma'jil* in the centre.

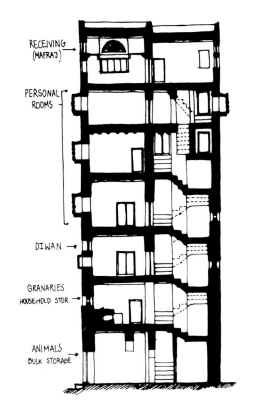

RECEIVING (MAFRAJ)

PERSONAL ROOMS

DIWAN

GRANARIES
HOUSEHOLD STOR.

ANIMALS
BULK STORAGE

# 3. THE HOUSE

A major variation of the tower house contains a top floor courtyard with light wells *(shamsiya)* for the lower floors. The origins of this sub-type are not certain, but it may be pre-Islamic: it occurs densely in areas influenced by the *himyaritic* kingdoms, and in the urban homes built by the Jews in the oldest part of San͑a' — later adapted for segregated Jewish quarters.

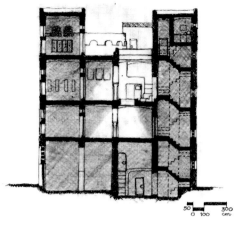

*(Opposite) Top:* Sections of mud house *(left)* and large stone house *(right)* with top courts and light wells in Dhamar. *Centre Right:* Light well extending from top court to ground floor with circulation galleries around, Kawkaban. *Centre Left:* Top courts and light wells, Thula. *Bottom Right:* Top light for kitchen and circulation areas in a rural house, Bani Qaysh. *Bottom Left:* Top light holes, Kawkaban.

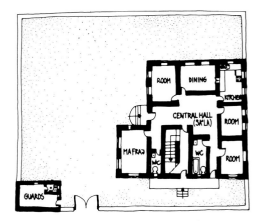

With the end of the Civil War, new house types were introduced: urban apartment buildings built in concrete up to four storeys high and single family houses modelled on the 'villa', with one or two storeys, stone walls, a concrete frame, a central-corridor plan and a large garden surrounded by a high wall. In the countryside a hybrid type developed primarily for emigrants and the new middle class, with the ground floor used as living quarters. The change in social and economic status identified with these houses is reflected in the somewhat disordered ornamental display, both in colour and texture.

*Top Right:* Plan of 'villa', San<sup>c</sup>a'. *Centre Right:* Cement and stone apartment buildings in the main commercial street of San<sup>c</sup>a' built after the Revolution. *Centre Left:* A villa in San<sup>c</sup>a'. *Bottom:* A new house on the outskirts of Rada<sup>c</sup>, using traditional elements of construction but a different spatial organisation (living quarters also on the ground floor).

# 3. THE HOUSE

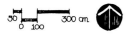

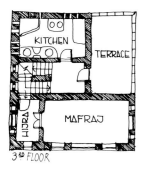

3ʳᵈ FLOOR

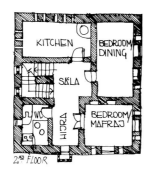

2ⁿᵈ FLOOR

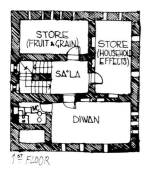

1ˢᵗ FLOOR

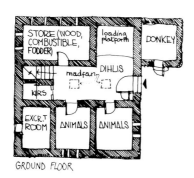

GROUND FLOOR

Although the distinction between rural and urban houses may be apparent in their external aspect, it is as evident in the allocation of interior space. Rural houses allow more space for functions directly related to rural activities, while urban houses allot more space for living quarters, not only for the family but also for the reception of visitors, an important part of social life.

Patterns of use vary with social practice. In the rural areas both men and women work in the fields; women also carry out the household chores. In both rural and urban areas men do the shopping in the morning. In the afternoons men and women socialise separately, visiting (especially in cities), chewing *qat*, smoking the water pipe, drinking *qishr*, tea, etc. Women move into the husband's house on marriage, returning to the father's house if widowed or divorced. In rural areas the married son often builds his own house, although larger houses of more wealthly families may contain three generations and several family units, each

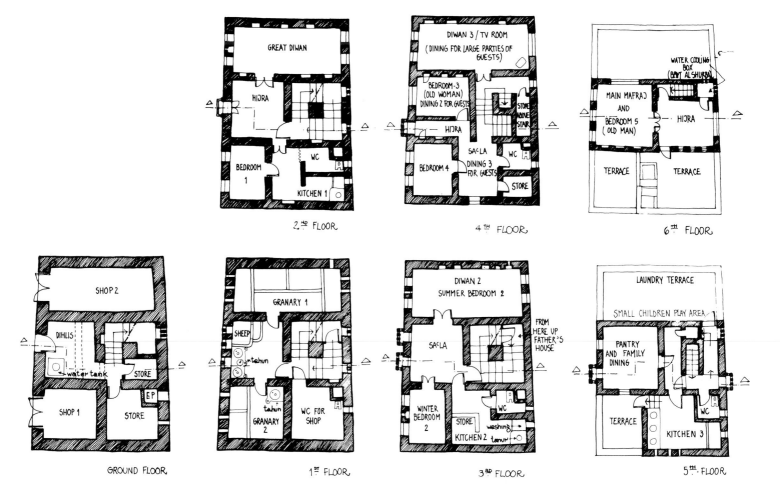

family unit having its own room or storey and sharing certain communal rooms. The best rooms are usually reserved for the oldest members of the household; being the best lit and ventilated they may also be used as sleeping rooms for the very young. In such extended family groups women usually share the household chores, although there may be more than one kitchen to minimise conflict.

In the houses of the Highlands circulation and service areas face north, but the best rooms face south. This orientation changes in the south and in Tihama because of the heat. Even in large houses in the Highlands room-use frequently changes according to the season: thus people sleep in the warmest rooms during winter though these rooms may be used for different purposes the rest of the year.

The hierarchy of space within the house may be further articulated by different floor treatments. Thus in stone, stone and brick, and some mud houses, circulation and service areas may be paved with stone slabs, whereas the

stables and stores on the ground floor are left with an earthen floor. Living rooms may be surfaced with a mixture of plaster, coal and alabaster powder *(qdad)*, sometimes brightly polished, and covered with straw mats and rugs or, more recently, with linoleum. Terraces may be finished with water-resistant lime plaster.

The difference between circulation zones (where shoes are worn) and living rooms (where shoes are taken off) is often emphasised by the raising of door thresholds, defining the beginning of the living quarters. Doors are low (some being only 1.3 m. high, while a door higher than 1.7 m. is rare) and the head must be bent on entering and leaving. *Top Right:* Detail of door. *Below:* Schematic plan of floor treatment in a house in at-Tawila.

*(Opposite) Top:* Plan of a semi-rural house in at-Tawila with stable annex and *madfan* (underground area for grain storage). *Bottom:* Plan of a house with shops in San^c a' near Suq al-Milh.

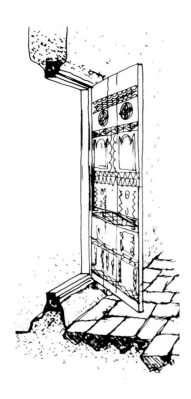

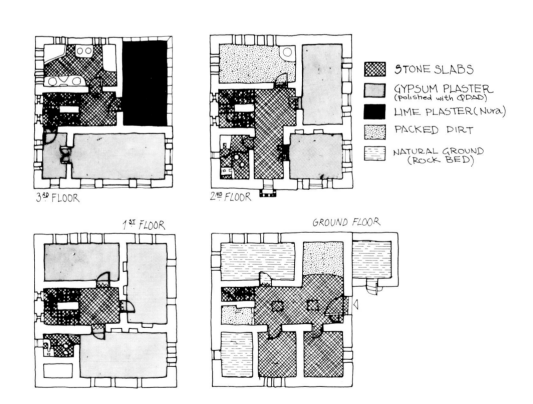

STONE SLABS

GYPSUM PLASTER
(polished with QDAD)

LIME PLASTER (Nura)

PACKED DIRT

NATURAL GROUND
(ROCK BED)

3RD FLOOR

2ND FLOOR

1ST FLOOR

GROUND FLOOR

# 3. THE HOUSE

The main door of the house may open to a small front yard (where the well is often located) or directly onto the street. It usually receives special treatment in the form of elaborate wood carvings or just a small embellishment on the iron door knocker. Stone buildings usually display a reticulated tympanum (to ventilate and light the entrance hall) which is a distinctive feature of the facade. The door may be wide enough to allow the passage of loaded animals with a smaller opening in the main panel for people. *Top Left:* Door with simple tympanum, Saᶜda. *Top Centre:* Reticulated tympanum, Sanᶜa'.

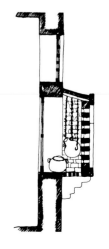

The *shubaq* is a perforated casement window of mud, stone, brick or wood lattice from which women can observe the street without being seen. It is thus located in the circulation and service areas most frequented by women. The *shubaq* is also the place where drinking water is left to cool in porous earthenware jars. *Centre Right:* Shubaq in terrace, hallways and cooling box *(foreground), Sanᶜa'. Bottom Left:* Door and stone *shubaq,* Khamir. *Bottom Centre:* Schematic section of *shubaq.*

The ground floor contains a lofty entrance hall *(dihliz)*, stables and store rooms for farm equipment and fodder. A small sheep pen or chicken coop *(kirs)* may be under the main staircase to the upper floors. There is also a small compartment to collect excrement from the toilets for later use as fertiliser. A loading platform and another for hand feeding animals are often at the entrance. Rural houses may contain a *madfan*. The ground level of houses near the market is often used for shops. Until recently every house had its grinding mills *(tahun, mathana)*; although following the intro-

duction of motorised mills in the 1950s the grinding stones are rarely or never used. The mill is usually found in a special place on the first floor or half-floor (in San<sup>c</sup>a' the first floor is commonly a mezzanine), though it may be on the ground floor in the entrance hall or under the staircase. Larger kitchens may also have a mill. Masonry storage bins for grain or fruit are to be found in the *tabaqat al-habb* on the first floor or mezzanine. *Top Right: Tahun,* Mithal. *Top Left:* Rural entrance hall, Tana<sup>c</sup>im. *Bottom Right: Tabaqat al-habb,* San<sup>c</sup>a'. *Bottom Left: Tahun,* Yarim.

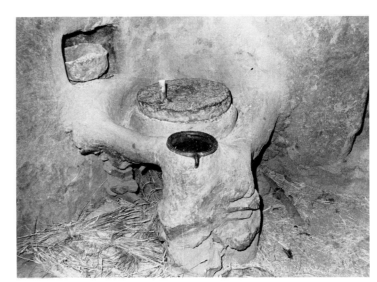

## 3. THE HOUSE

The stairs lead from the ground to the top floor around a stone newel *(qutb),* the solid backbone of the house. Steps are made of stone or mud in short runs with corner landings. Finished stone steps average 25 cm. riser and 25 cm. tread. Most stairs are lit and ventilated by reticulated windows at the landings that constitute, together with the *shubaq,* the cross ventilation system of the house. However, in rural areas, steps may be very irregular and lit badly or not at all. *Top Right:* Mud stairs and ventilation holes, Rada<sup>c</sup>. *Below Centre:* Examples of stairwells. *Below Left:* Mud stairs, Sa<sup>c</sup>da. *Bottom Right:* Stone stairs, Ibb. *Bottom Left:* Mud stairs and stone arches, Mithal.

*(Opposite):* Ventilation holes in stair of large stone house, Hajja.

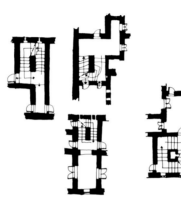

# 3. THE HOUSE

The second floor, sometimes also the third floor, contains additional store rooms, household pantries and the largest room in the house, the *diwan*. The *diwan* is a reception room for special functions such as weddings, births or funerals. It is also the room where tribesmen meet to deliberate tribal matters and sometimes hold court. Because of structural limitations the average width of the *diwan* is 3 m.; however, it may run the whole length of the house. When not in use, it is unfurnished and may function as a store room or seasonal bedroom. Larger houses may contain more than one *diwan,* while in smaller houses the functions of the *diwan* are distributed among other living rooms.

The ceilings of certain areas in the house (the bathroom, kitchen, hallway, etc.) may be lowered to create additional storage space. Secret storerooms where food and valuables are protected from ransackers may be hidden between double walls or under floors. This practice is particularly evident in the Jewish houses of San<sup>c</sup>a'. *Below Right:* Secret storage spaces *(shaded areas)* connected to main store rooms by trap doors. The storage areas above the stair landings are also shaded. *Below Left:* Storage room, San<sup>c</sup>a'. *Bottom: Diwan* of sheikh's house, Ta<sup>c</sup>la, Sahar. Only half the room is shown.

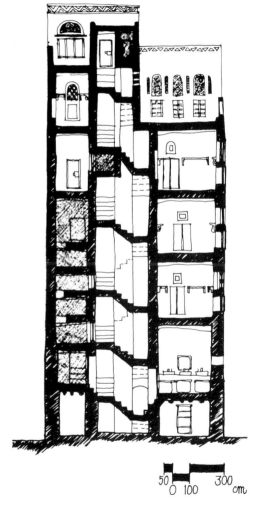

Each floor has an unfurnished hall *(hijra* or *saᶜla)* which may be a wide landing in the stairs or a room separated from the stairs by a door. This hall is a passageway or antechamber where waterpipes are lit and shoes taken off at the entrance of the rooms. The *saᶜla* is a hallway customarily used as a dining area. These hallways are usually equipped with a *shubaq. Centre: Shubaq in hijra,* Bi'r al-ᶜAzab, Sanᶜa'. *Top Left: Hijra* antechamber of *mafraj,* at-Tawila. *Bottom: Saᶜla,* Thula.

# 3. THE HOUSE

The upper floors of the tower house, containing the sleeping rooms, sitting rooms, dining areas, kitchens and bathrooms, are the most private. Men are generally not allowed in areas frequented by women; to avoid encounters on their way to the reception rooms they announce their presence on the stairs by crying out 'allah, allah'. This warns the women to close the doors between hall and stair or move to their rooms. Although a couple may share a room, it is common for women with children to occupy a room separate from the husband. When there is more than one wife,

each has her own room. The oldest man and women have the best and second best rooms for their personal use, the latter functioning also as the women's *mafraj*. Family sitting rooms may be known as *al-istiqbal* or *al-majmu'a* (gathering rooms). All living rooms are furnished in the same way, most simply by rugs on the floor and some cushions. Complete traditional furnishing consists of rugs *(mafrasha)*, floor mattresses along the walls *(farsh)*, hard cushions for the back *(wusada)*, arm rests *(madka)* and small soft cushions which are placed on top of the back cushions or arm rests *(mukhada* or

*bint al-wusada)*. The centre of the floor may be covered with rugs or, today, colourful patterned linoleum.

Clothes or personal effects are kept in trunks and chests, hung from large iron or wooden pegs in the walls, or placed in plaster shelves *(sfaf)* or in niches with or without doors *(maqhfara, sunduq)*. Sleeping rooms usually double as sitting or dining areas. Usually, no room is designated solely as the dining room; the family may eat in any room, the hallway or the pantry. Formal guests dine in the main *mafraj*, large parties in the *diwan* and hallways.

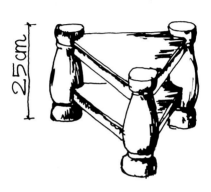

*Top:* Lunch served on floor, Barat. *Bottom Right:* Sitting/dining room, al-Haraka, Rada^c. Note the lamp hook and chain hanging from the ceiling. *Bottom Left:* Stone oil lamp. Now obsolete, such lamps of stone or alabaster were hung from the ceiling. Each point had a wick. Today houses are lit with kerosene or primus lamps, or neon tubes if electricity is available.

*(Opposite) Centre Right:* Niches in sleeping/sitting room, Dhamar. *Centre Left:* Wooden and metal tea trays found in at-Tawila and San^ca' respectively. *Bottom Right:* Typically furnished *mafraj*, Wadi Dahr. *Bottom Left;* Sleeping room, Sa^cda.

## 3. THE HOUSE

The most privileged rooms in the house are the *mafraj* or *manzar* (the root of both words refers to a 'good view'). The *mafraj* is generally a large room (12-18 sq. m. in area) that may be located on the top floor, while the *manzar* is a separate attic at the top of the house exclusively reserved for the house owner and his special guests.

*Qat*-chewing is one of the most important Yemeni traditions. The leaf from the bush *(catha edulis)*, freshly cut and then chewed, has a euphoric effect. It is probably true that every afternoon every adult Yemeni chews *qat* — in shops, while working, walking in the streets, or driving. However, the *mafraj* and *manzar* are rooms specially designed for the purpose. Afternoons are spent here chewing *qat*, talking, listening to music, smoking the waterpipe *(madaᶜa)*, and looking at the view and the patterns of the coloured glass fanlights. In the Highlands *qat*-chewing starts after lunch and lasts until evening. The session begins with light conversation and discussion (tribal deliberations are heard at this stage). Singers and dancers may perform for the guests, though now recorded music is more common. *Below: Qat* session, Sanᶜa'. Bundles of *qat*, thermos bottles, spitoons and the long-hosed waterpipe can be seen.

*(Opposite) Mafraj* at *qat* time.

## 3. THE HOUSE

Ablution *(masfa)* and toilet facilities are usually near the receiving rooms. The *masfa* may be in the antechamber, at one end of a sitting/sleeping room, or on the roof. Some provide space for prayer. The bathroom consists of a stone or mud latrine, a washing area, a large water container, and a shallow trough which channels liquid waste outside. Liquid and solid waste are separated. In tall houses, liquid waste flows down a surface waterproofed with lime plaster *(nura)*, evaporating before it reaches the ground. Mud houses may use a drainpipe which juts out from the wall. Low houses have a drainage sump to collect the waste. In the east and south-east solid waste from the latrine falls down an inclined stone to the outside where it quickly dries. In the Highlands and the Old Town of San'a' solid waste is used as fuel (for the public *hammam*) and then fertiliser (as ashes). Elsewhere human excrement is used as manure. The introduction of domestic piped water before an alternative sewage system was devised has unfortunately resulted in 'open sewers'. *Below Right:* Top floor plan of house in San'a' with full bath serving top *manzar. Below Centre:* Top floor plan of house in al-Hanaka with *masfa* in *mafraj* antechamber. *Below Left: Masfa* at one end of sleeping/sitting room, Suq al-'Ainan, Barat. *Bottom:* Bathroom/ toilet, in Hajja. *(Right)* and *Sa'da (Left).*

*(Opposite): Top Right:* Schematic section and plan of bathroom/toilet, showing stepped construction permitting toilets on each level to use a single sanitary shaft. *Top Centre:* Protruding sanitary shaft with toilet at the top, Barat. *Top Left:* Excrement-collecting chamber, at-Tawila. *Bottom Right:* New piping replacing traditional waterproofed drainage surface, Sa'da. *Bottom Left:* Waterproofed drainage surface, Rada'.

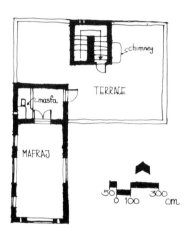

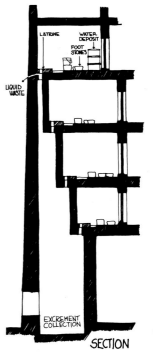

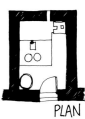

LATRINE

WATER
DEPOSIT

FOOT
STONES

LIQUID
WASTE

EXCREMENT
COLLECTION

SECTION

PLAN

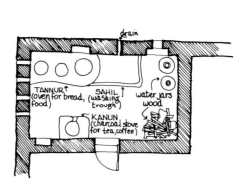

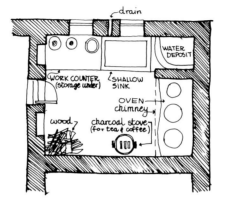

Kitchens are bare of comfort and poorly lit. They are often located on the top floor to allow direct ventilation through the ceiling, with other holes in the smoke-blackened walls. Kitchens in the lower floors may have a crude chimney, a parapet above the stove and a flue carrying smoke up to the roof. Cooking is done in a mud oven lined with baked clay *(tannur)*. There is a lateral hole near the bottom for fuel where ashes can be drawn out. Food is prepared on a ledge or on the floor. Washing is done in a shallow trough *(sahil)* lined in stone or lime plaster and set on a ledge or the floor. At one end of the trough is a large water jar or masonry container. Tea and coffee are prepared in a small stove, portable or built-in *(kanun)*, whose coals are used to light the waterpipe. Fuel and utensils are stored in the kitchen, but not food. *Top Right:* Woman at work in the kitchen. *Top Centre:* Plans of two kitchens. *Centre Right:* Oven with arch and chimney, Wadi Dahr, showing design influence from Jewish kitchens in Sanᶜa'. *Bottom Right:* Kitchen, at-Tawila. *Bᴑttom Left:* Kitchen trough and wood fuel, Saᶜda.

The roof terrace is also a service area. Here room furnishings are dusted and cleaned, clothes are dried, and herbs are grown. Terraces are used mostly by women and often have a *shubaq* in the parapet walls. Terraces protected by walls are also play areas for small children. When chimneys occur they are no higher than the roof level. They have a variety of shapes with multiple perforations, the simplest form being a triangular cover with two tiles. *From Top Right to Bottom Left:* Chimneys in al-Kitba, and Sanᶜa' (the most common type); terraces in Thula, Saᶜda and Sanᶜa'.

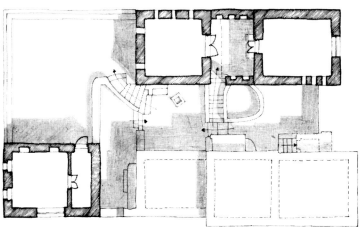

# 4. THE ART OF BUILDING

*'All Yemenis are architects'* (Elliott Roberts)

*'The country lies over a complex of metamorphic rocks, probably pre-Cambrian in origin, consisting chiefly of mica, schists, gneisses, quartzites and marbles across which run intrusions of massive granite and basaltic dykes. Overlaying these are Jurassic beds and tertiary rocks consisting of cretaceous sandstones, volcanic tuffs, basalts and andesites. The most recent are the alluvial formations of the plains in the centre of the country and coastal plains of the Tihama.'*
(Central Planning Organisation Statistical Year Book, 1975)

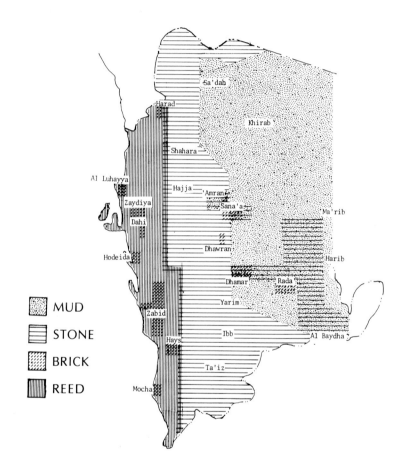

Regional construction generally conforms to landscape and geological structure. Thus, mud construction is characteristic of the east and central-east, with pockets in the plains and plateaux of the Highlands and Midlands; in these latter regions stone architecture — limestone and lava in the north and centre, granite in the south, schist in the south-east — predominates. Baked brick is found in the largest centres of the mountains, combined with or adjacent to mud and stone construction, and in the major interior towns of Tihama alongside reed houses.

Though there is regional variation in wall construction, the construction of roofs and foundations is everywhere the same — with the exception of the Tihama reed houses.

Farmers build their several-storey houses with the help of family and neighbours, and tribesmen assist in the construction of their sheikh's houses. In major towns the house building is often entrusted to specialists, giving a diverse set of craftsmen an opportunity to elaborate on certain aspects. When the first arch of the house is built, the owner, faithful to tradition, sacrifices a sheep and marks the house with blood as a prophylactic measure. When the house is completed a celebration takes place where learned men (*ʿulama*) are invited to recite verses of the Koran.

100

## Crafts Organisation

Among the various craftsmen involved in house construction (for instance, in San‘a’), the main role belongs unquestionably to the *usta*, the chief mason and contractor who is responsible for the whole building. The corporation of masons is very hierarchical and the erection of a simple wall demands no less than three classes of masons. First of all the *usta* is responsible for laying the facade stones (*wajh*), the first ones to be placed. The *thana* (from *tny* 'to double') then lays the first row of stones for the internal face of the wall. Finally, the *rassas* fills in the wall with stone chips and mud mortar to which gypsum plaster is sometimes added. A day-labourer (*shaqi*) supplies the stones. Thus, to the various tasks correspond various degrees of competence and it is not easy to pass from one category to another.

How does one become a *usta*? Without being strictly hereditary, access to the title of *usta* requires not only professional experience but also the patronage of a qualified *usta*. For several years a young mason will work under the guidance of his father, his uncle or another *usta* who has taken him under his protection. Gradually the pupil (*tilmidh*) begins to work on his own, first from a construction site under the patronage and name of his master (*muallim*), until he in turn becomes a recognised *usta* able to engrave his name on the house he has finished. The *usta* works for the owner of the building either on a wage basis (*ujra*), in which case he re-distributes to his masons and workers the weekly pay that the owner gives him, or by becoming a contractor (*muqawwil*) for the whole.

Bricks for the construction are bought directly from the kilns. Stones are purchased at the quarry through the services of an intermediary who transports them (today by lorry) and sells them by the truckload (*zaffa*) to the owner of the house or to the *usta* if he is the contractor. Cutting the stones (*waqis*) is the responsibility of the *muwaqqis* who works at the construction site directed by the *usta*. The *muwaqqis* often works in a team. He is paid by the piece according to the form of the stone (*hajar wajh*: facade stone; *dubr:* angle stone; *mardam:* sill stone; *galfa:* roughly cut stone for the interior side of the wall) and the nature of the rock (*abyad, ahmar, habash*). He receives a money advance adjusted in each phase of construction by patiently counting the stones of the various types once they are put in their place. If he works hard a *muwaqqis* may earn a good living but he never attains the prestige of the *usta*.

Once the house is finished, other craftsmen make their appearance. First comes the plasterer (*muqassis*) and his team, who are responsible for all gypsum plaster work (*guss*), not only the surfacing of walls and ceilings but also the construction of plaster shelves (*safif*) and especially the fretwork (*takhrim*) for the fanlights (*‘uqud*). Next is the carpenter. Houses may be left for several months without windows and doors until the owner accumulates enough money to proceed to the carpentry for the doors, windows and *kunna*, the traditional ornamented board above the windows.

Houses which traditionally had floors of plaster later covered with rugs or mats are now being floored with terrazzo tiles. The tile-layer (*ballat*) is a highly qualified craftsman who may have previously specialised in *qadad* (the lime-plaster surfacing used on mosque domes, bath house walls and sometimes in the hallways of wealthy houses). To complete today's house an electrician, plumber and cesspool digger (*ballu'a*) are called in — the latter a traditional, particularly hard, but well paid job.

# 4. THE ART OF BUILDING

The building is constructed from the ground level up, so that no scaffolding is required. When work is needed high up on the external face of the wall, a platform is hung from ropes held on the roof by one or two men. Tools are few and used only for certain techniques in stone, carpentry and the making of plaster screens for the fanlights. Construction work in mud, plastering, etc., is done mostly with bare hands.

There is a certain nonchalance in the way construction materials are treated; this is probably why plumbing and wiring are so *ad hoc*. The house receives atten-

tion according to the status of its user and its embellishment is merely a question of degree, following the same principles and themes as used in weaving and carving: weaving a pattern of Vs or lozenges in a wool rug and inlaying the same designs in a brick or stone frieze follow similar methods. *Top:* Window frame with burglar bars mounted in stone wall under construction, Dumran. *Bottom Left:* Mud construction, Khirab. A man kneads mud with his feet as another layer of mud is placed on top of the building. *Bottom Right:* Plastering around a window, Saᶜda.

102

Foundations, often laid on *wadi* boulders, are made from basalt or other hard rock if basalt is not available. With improved transportation, however, basalt is now widely used in regions where previously it was not part of the building tradition. Depth of foundations is empirically determined: the ground is dug until only the tip of the pick makes an impression. In practice this allows a wide safety margin, any error usually being by excess. The foundation may end at ground level or extend for several stone courses until it dissolves into the stone walls of the ground floor. *Top:* Mud wall and stone foundation merging with the stone door frame, al-Qaᶜ, Sanᶜa'. *Bottom:* Stone foundation running into the stone of the ground floor, Dhamar.

# 4. THE ART OF BUILDING

Stone is taken from the quarries in large blocks that are later cut at the construction site. Improved transportation has made quarries more accessible; as a result, stone is now appearing in areas where mud was once the only building material, and stone from different quarries is being used on the same site. *Top:* The ground floor is of rough local stone while differently-cut stone from another area is used for the windows and upper floors, al-Mawra. *Bottom Right:* Stone wall, al-Hajra. *Bottom Left:* Wood joists embedded in the wall work as lintels and load distributors, al-Uda ͨyn.

*(Opposite)* Various types of stone treatment.

# 4. THE ART OF BUILDING

The treatment of the external wall face varies according to region and preference. Cut stone is finished by degree — ¼ cut, ½ cut, full cut. The most polished cutting is seen especially in San‛a', Dhamar, and their areas of influence. When the full cut is perfectly executed the joints must coincide so precisely that light does not pass through. Today, small imperfections are often covered by a thin layer of gypsum plaster over the joint. Stone may not require mortar, or may use a mortar made with mud to which lime or gypsum may be added. In some regions, mainly in the south, a mortar is made with lime and earth, the joints being underlined with lime. In the mountains the internal wall is surfaced with plaster made of mud, straw and sometimes dung: this is also used for the sub-surfacing of ceilings *(malaj)*. Whenever possible, the final wall surface is of gypsum plaster which is also an efficient insulator. Modern construction has largely abandoned the sub-surfacing of walls with mud plaster. *Top:* Tools. *Centre:* Selecting, cutting and laying the stone. *Bottom:* Interior wall ready to be plastered; full cut stone wall; fixing the plumb line.

Arches are widely used in stone constructions for openings and to cover large rooms with spans of up to 6 m. The arch frame is filled with mud or baked bricks, or, more recently, cement blocks. Increasing use of iron bars in windows has led to another method: the top of the bars is cut in an arch shape and the stones are laid with this as a frame. Arches may be embedded in tall building walls to distribute loads, a function also performed by wood logs or joists *(basut)* which often serve as the lintel between the upper and lower part of a window. Though concrete has become popular since its appearance in the mid-1960s, stone is still the most prestigious building material. Concrete is used with stone for foundations and roof slabs. The combination of concrete frame and load bearing walls, unnecessarily duplicating the structure, has not so far been successfully resolved. *Top Right:* Arched door. *Centre Right:* Using burglar bars to make an arch, San'a'. *Centre Left:* Arch, Sirha. *Bottom Left and Above:* Making arches for windows.

# 4. THE ART OF BUILDING

Mud construction follows three main methods: clay courses *(zabur)* 50-60 cm. high, adobe blocks *(libn)*, and baked bricks *(yajur)*. *Zabur* is found everywhere in the Highlands, at least for orchard and garden walls, but it is best utilised in the north and north-east where it is almost the only method of building. Earth from the construction site is soaked in water, kneaded and mixed with straw, and thrown in a ball-shape to the master builder who slaps it down onto the course under construction. The mud course is then hand-shaped by other workers and finally finished with a spatula. Intersections are made at the same time even if the whole wall is only later completed. For structural reasons the walls are tapered to the inside and the corners are raised. The clay courses may be left exposed or covered with mud plaster. *Below: Zabur* in Saᶜda.

*(Opposite) Zabur* construction in process. *Bottom Right:* Khirab. *Bottom Left:* Saᶜda.

# 4. THE ART OF BUILDING

Sun-dried blocks are found alongside *zabur* constructions in the north, and elsewhere frequently co-exist with stone and brick constructions either as an independent architectural form or as subsidiary material for interior walls, etc. *Libn* blocks are made of clay mixed with straw (preferably barley), set in wood moulds and left to dry. Dimensions vary — 40 x 25 x 12 cm. in the area around San<sup>c</sup>a' and 35 x 30 x 10 cm. in the area around Dhamar. Baked bricks are smaller — in San<sup>c</sup>a' the full size is 16 x 16 x 4 cm. and the half size

is 16 x 8 x 4 cm. These are left to dry in the sun and baked in slow-burning kilns for one week, after which they are left inside another two days to cool. In some walls, the wall interior is made of *libn,* smaller half-size baked bricks being used for the facing. *Top Right:* Sun-dried brick wall with moulded mud cyma, al-Hanaka. *Centre and Bottom Right:* Making bricks in wooden moulds. *Centre Left and Middle:* Brick kilns, San<sup>c</sup>a'. *Bottom Left:* Bricks drying in the sun.

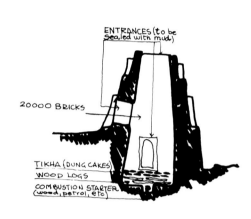

Affinities between decorative patterns in architecture and various crafts are evident. Patterns are 'woven' into brick and stone walls, as they are woven in basketry and rugs; motifs are 'carved' into plaster and wood as they are carved in jewellery; wall paintings, too, are reminiscent of painted ceramics. *Top:* Zaydyia. *Below Right:* Wool vest with geometric patterns and Koranic inscription *(Ma sha'Allah:* The will of God be done) often appearing in wall decorations. *Bottom Left:* Brick wall, San<sup>c</sup>a'.

# 4. THE ART OF BUILDING

Domed roofs are reserved for certain religious and funerary buildings. House roofs are flat and normally solid enough to be the floor of an upper storey. In some simple one-storey structures the roof may be made of stone slabs supported by arches or tree-trunks. Most commonly, however, the roof consists of a frame of wooden beams set 50-60 cm. apart,

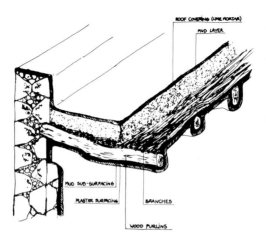

covered by branches and twigs, on top of which lie layers of finely sifted earth, wet and compact, up to a thickness of 30 cm. Ceilings are usually plastered with gypsum on top of a mud sub-surfacing. *Top:* Schematic detail of roof. *Centre:* Purlins, Sacda. *Bottom Right:* Sub-surfacing of a ceiling with mud, Sanca'. *Bottom Left:* Roof under construction, Sanca'.

Room width is of course conditioned by the maximum length of the tree purlins, varying between 2.0 and 3.5 m. Although local wood purlins are selected from the straightest trees, some irregularity is unavoidable and this often creates an interesting volumetric play in the plastered ceiling. Scarcity of timber has become critical, particularly after the Civil War and the construction boom that followed. Wood joists are now being imported, but so far this has not increased the average room span though it has tended to standardise room sizes within the 3.2 - 3.5 m. span. Imported joists are usually more regular, being pre-cut, and are often left exposed. *Top:* Plastered ceiling, an-Nadira. *Bottom:* Exposed imported joists, Ibb.

## 4. THE ART OF BUILDING

The rendering of external surfaces around windows, domes and roof terraces is traditionally done with lime plaster (qadad, nura) also used for interior surfacing in areas where lime was more accessible than gypsum. *Nura* or *qadad* is also used to provide a waterproof surface in bathrooms, hallways and stairs, where it is rubbed until shiny with powdered alabaster and cow grease. This slow, highly specialised process is now rarely practised in the mountains. Modern transport has made gypsum more easily available and it is now widely used in the fretwork for fanlights and in interiors where it is easily incised into elaborate decorative patterns. In more remote rural houses, where lime and gypsum plaster are still luxuries, walls are surfaced in mud with simple moulded decorative motifs. *Top:* Rendering around windows, Saʿda. *Centre Right and Bottom: Nura* carvings in mosque domes, Sanʿa'. *Centre Left: Nura* carving in mosque dome, Hadda.

*Top Right: Nura* carving in hallway waterproofed with alabaster and cow grease, San'a'. *Top Left: Nura* carving, Ta'la, Sahar. *Centre Right:* Gypsum plaster carving, Kawkaban. *Centre Left:* Carving patterns in gypsum plaster around a window, San'a'. *Bottom Right:* Photos inset into plaster wall, al-Jihana. *Bottom Left:* Hammam 'Ali.

*(Overleaf)* Traditional *takhrim* designs.

# 4. THE ART OF BUILDING

In general windows have two distinct parts: the lower opening *(taqa)* offers a view and provides ventilation, and may also be a light source; separated from this by a lintel is an upper fixed section of alabaster or glass which provided an additional source of light when defence considerations made the size of the lower opening minimal. In time this upper section developed into a fanlight *('aqd, 'uqud)*, becoming more important as a light source and decorative element. Ventilation holes *(shaqus)* may be placed between fanlights. Fanlights consisting of small pieces of alabaster in designs of superimposed circles, combinations of circles and small arches (sometimes called *qamariya*: from *qamar*, the moon) are found in the oldest houses and most distant areas. The use of rectangular alabaster plates in arched openings occurs later. These plates have a regular size to fit most openings; when larger windows are required, as in a top floor *mafraj*, small plates are mounted in a stone or brick frame (larger plates being rarely found), or a plaster fretwork *(takhrim)* is used to complement or replace the alabaster, being regarded as an improvement over the original. (As a result of urban influence alabaster is now often replaced by glass panes.) *Takhrim* may be of wood (Ta'izz, Dharawan), but most commonly it consists of a pattern of stucco tracery filled in with different coloured glass pieces. In its most developed form it has two panes with different designs, the exterior one decorating the facade being colourless: the superimposition of the exterior and interior panels varying with the light creates a fascinating play of coloured patterns. A piece of white cloth may be stretched between the panes to reduce the glare. *Takhrim* are found in a great variety of designs and styles, and different phases can be observed: intricate geometric patterns, with thin nervures and small pieces of brightly coloured glass; calligraphic treatment of Koranic inscriptions; freer forms with larger surfaces of more palely coloured glass. Lately plasterwork has become so rich that it dominates the glass colour combinations; most recently there has been a return to more strictly geometrical patterns. Figurative representations, traditionally reduced to the stylisation of floral elements, appear more overtly after the Revolution either in the recurring theme of the Republican eagle or in other motifs deriving from the Civil War — planes, weapons, cars.

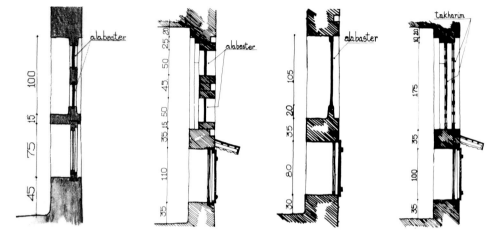

*Top, from Right to Left:* Alabaster fanlights with multiple panes in Shibam al-Aqyan, Dhamar and San͑a'. *Centre:* Building showing fretwork from various periods in San͑a'. *Bottom Right and Centre:* Post-Revolution themes, an-Nadira. *Bottom Left: Takhrim* with Koranic inscription, San͑a'.

*(Opposite) Top:* Schematic sections of four window types with fanlights. *Bottom Right:* Alabaster fanlight in stone, Mithal al-Hada'. *Bottom Left:* Multiple alabaster fanlight in mud, Rada͑.

119

To make *takhrim* a thick layer of gypsum plaster is spread in the shape of the opening onto a board placed against a wall. The surface is smoothed with a trowel; the basic design is drawn with a compass and/or pointer and cut before it hardens. Once dry, the frame is separated from the board, turned over and again laid on the board. Glass is cut, put in place and sprinkled with a very liquid plaster to adhere to the frame. As this dries, a thicker layer of plaster is poured over it, again smoothed with a trowel and cut out against the light so that the design can be followed. The panel is then mounted in the openings and fixed with plaster.

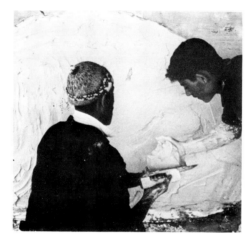

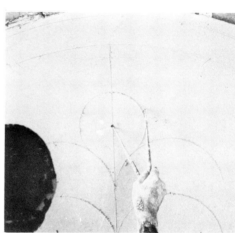

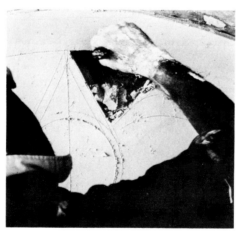

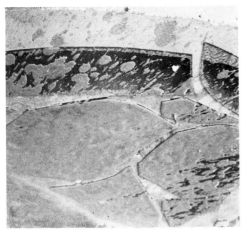

# 4. THE ART OF BUILDING

Skilled carpentry in doors and windows is now rare, because of the scarcity of wood and the exodus of the Jewish craftsmen largely responsible for this craft as also for jewellery and fretwork. However, examples of their high quality work remain. In the south (Taᶜizz) and Tihama, carpentry shows the influence of Indian workmanship. Windows usually had opening shutters in each of the panes to allow greater control of light and air without losing privacy. *Top, Bottom Right and Bottom Left, in order:* Door exteriors in Taᶜizz, Ibb and Saᶜda.

*(Opposite) Top Right and Centre:* Traditional lock, al-Sabahi. The key pushes up the bodkin from the side. *Top Left:* Window with mother-of-pearl inlay, Thula. *Centre Right:* Locks, padlocks and keys. *Bottom Right:* Door interior, Kawkaban. *Bottom Left:* Door exterior with metal knocker, Sadda.

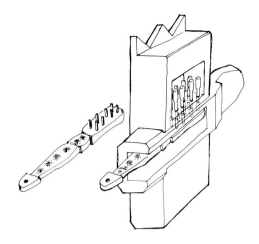

# 4. THE ART OF BUILDING

Window gratings in wood, gypsum or lime plaster, still visible in various parts of the country, are a form of protecting the house and the children inside (windows are rarely more than 40 cm. from the floor). These gratings, like wooden lattices, are now being replaced by parallel iron bars. *Top, Bottom Right and Bottom Left, in order:* Wooden window gratings in Dhamar, al-Bayda' and al-Mahabisha.

Turkish influence in the mountains is seen in a number of wooden overhanging balconies, also seen in profusion in coastal towns. Later structures show a simpler design and a more naive treatment. *Top, Right and Left:* Gypsum window gratings in Wadi Dahr and Sanᶜa'. *Centre Right:* Interior of Turkish balcony, Hajja. *Bottom Right:* Latticed casement in the style of a Turkish balcony, Sanᶜa'. *Bottom Left:* Elaborate Turkish balcony in Bi'r al-ᶜAzab, Sanᶜa'.

## 4. THE ART OF BUILDING

Coloured treatment of external walls, traditionally found only in eastern regions where mud building predominated, was confined to red ochre in bands along walls and around openings. Elsewhere, colour was provided only by interior furnishings and the *takhrim*. In Tihama, however, with its refined tradition of painted ceilings in Turkish houses, painted ceilings and painted furniture are common. One effect of the Revolution has been to provide ready access to industrial paint, leading to the painting in bright colours of all prized possessions — cars, motor cycles — and windows, walls and doors. The effect of improved transportation has meant that stones of different colours from distant quarries can be combined on the same site, and this type of facade ornamentation is becoming popular in cities and among the new middle classes. *Top:* Cushions in *mafraj,* al-Mahwit. *Bottom:* Curtains and fanlights produce rich colour effects in this *mafraj,* al-Qaᶜ, Sanᶜa'.

*(Opposite) Top:* Window decorated with new enamel-painted designs, at-Tawila. *Bottom:* Decoration in enamel paint on new stone rural house, near al-Hawyin.

External wall painting on stone houses may display the same motifs that women throughout the country paint on their bodies — spots, dots and strokes. Other motifs contain the same elements in inlaid work on stone and brick walls. White paintings are usually made of lime; occasionally black designs made of coal dust and grease appear. The best examples of painted walls are in the western and north-western Highlands, although white is commonly used everywhere to underline certain features of the facade. In the south-east, grey slate walls are often decorated with geometric motifs made in thicker plaster. *Bottom Right:* Black and white patterns cover the whole facade of this stone house in Hajja. *Left Side:* Women's hands and arms decorated in red or black patterns. Village women in some areas paint their faces a greasy yellow, green or blue as a form of sun protection, with black dots around eyebrows, nose and cheek.

*(Opposite) Top:* Delicate white patterns repeat motifs common in inlaid brickwork, al-Mahabisha. *Bottom:* Bolder designs on a mosque wall, Huth.

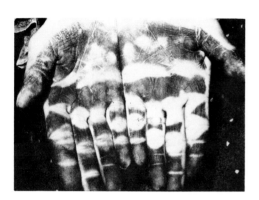

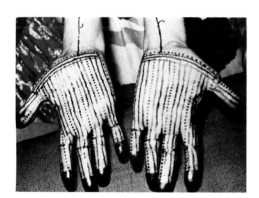

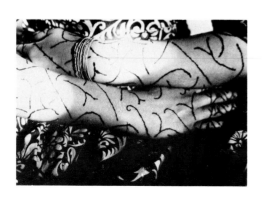

# 4. THE ART OF BUILDING

*Top:* Enamel painted wall in tea house, Saʿda. *Centre Right:* Enamel painted decoration of mud building in the old Jewish quarter, Dhamar. *Centre Left:* Old building with a new coat of plaster chequered with coloured wall paint, Sanʿa'. This manner of decoration was a passing fashion. *Bottom:* Coloured stone facades of modern houses in Sanʿa' *(right)* and Taʿizz *(left)*.

Refined results have been quickly achieved in the metal doors that have almost completely replaced wooden ones in new shops and houses. In ten years these have developed from simple wrought iron designs superimposed onto a painted metal sheet, to a repartition of the door surface in colours and forms reminiscent of the *takhrim*. *Top:* Metal door framed by painted mud wall on old building in Saᶜda. The wall was coated with cement before painting. *Below:* Types of metal gates. Except for the door from Dhi Bin *(centre of central row),* all examples are from Sanᶜa'. *Bottom Left:* The oldest example surveyed. *Bottom Right:* The most recent (under construction in 1976).

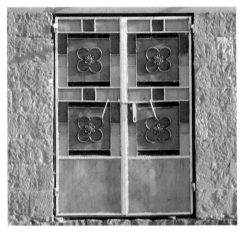

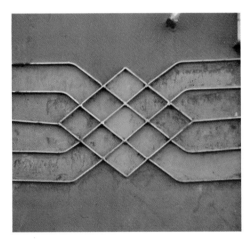

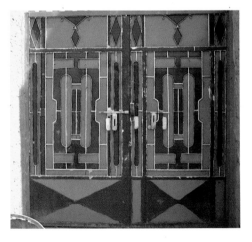

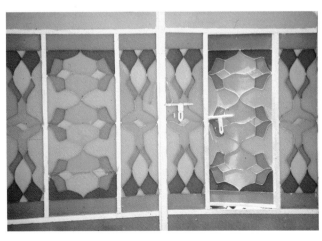

131

# PART TWO: REGIONAL SURVEYS

# 5. THE COASTAL STRIP (TIHAMA)

So far the coastal strip has been mentioned only in passing because, geographically and architecturally, it stands apart from the rest of the country. Known as Tihama (an ancient word found in Sabean inscriptions meaning 'low-lying country'), it consists of a semi-desert strip 30 to 70 km. wide between the mountains and the Red Sea. Geographically and culturally the region is as close to Africa as to the mountain heartland of Yemen. The population of fishermen and small farmers lives primarily in villages along the coast and the fertile irrigated areas along the *wadis*.

Reed and brick are the traditional building materials, though mud is often used with reed as a binding and insulating agent in interior finishing, or to create compound walls. Reed is used for market buildings and houses, which exist in great variety of plan (circular, rectangular), forms of roofing, methods of weaving fibres, interior and exterior surfacing, decoration, and general spatial organisation. Religious buildings are more monumental and are built in brick or stone masonry: white mosques or sanctuaries may be topped by several small brick domes.

Domestic architecture built of more durable material belongs to two groups. The first group is characteristic of the major towns south of al-Hudayda, represented by Zabid, once a great cultural and political centre. These houses are henceforth called Tihama brick houses. The second group is found in the major ports (al-Mukha, al-Luhayya, al-Hudayda) lived in by merchants and tradesmen, and ruled by an administrative elite closely connected to the Turkish rulers. These houses are built of brick or coral-rock and, as elsewhere along the shores of the Red Sea (Massawa in Ethiopia, Jeddah in Saudi Arabia, Suwakim in the Sudan) are known as Red Sea houses. *Top right:* Schematic distribution of major house types in Tihama. *Bottom right:* Women in al-Hudayda. *Bottom left:* Men in ath-Thawr.

(*Opposite*): Al-Jirb.

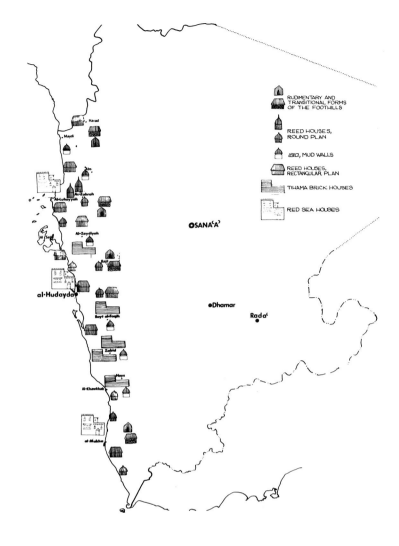

## 5. THE COASTAL STRIP

The foothills of Tihama are dotted with market places where local people and mountain people come weekly. Temporary markets are often open, or have only a small covered zone built of frail materials. Covered markets exist in reed and in masonry, the latter being found in the largest permanent markets, mainly in the southern half of the region. Market streets, covered with a variety of materials — flattened and rusty gallon cans as in Bayt al-Faqih, straw mats or twigs and palm leaves as in Hays, roofed over in galleries as in al-Jarrahi or Zabid -are the coolest places in the settlement and become the 'sitting place'.

At date-harvest time, when date festivals are held in some places, people camp for several days to harvest and feast. Ibn Battuta described such festivals in Zabid in the 14th century: *'The people of this city hold the famous* (junketings called) *"subut al nakhl" in this wise. They go out, during the season of the colouring and ripening of the dates, to the palmgroves on every Saturday. Not a soul remains in the town, whether of the townsfolk or of the strangers. The musicians go out* (to entertain them) *and the bazaar folk sell fruit and sweetmeats. The women go out riding on camels in litters.'*

*Right:* Market street, Hays, in southern Tihama. The covering of straw mats, palm leaves and discarded cartons makes the street cool.

*Top:* Suq al-Khamis, Bani Haij, Tihama — a lively open air market, one of the most important in the area. *Centre:* Reed market in the centre of al-Dahi, northern Tihama, a town with many brick buildings. *Bottom:* Market place in as-Suwayaq, near Zabid. In the midst of palm groves, this is the site of a date festival, hence the size of the market place.

Reed buildings of remarkable decorative invention are found throughout Tihama. The material may be reed, palm leaves, ropes made of palm fibres or sisal, grass or straw. The finish varies from loose 'grass' laid on top of a frame of branches and twigs to a woven fabric of straw and reed tied together with ropes in carefully designed geometric patterns. The structure is always the same: a strong frame of branches and vertical sticks, tied together at the apex (in the case of round huts), around which a secondary frame of flexible twigs is woven. The whole is then covered with fibres from roof-top to walls; the outer part of the wall may be surfaced with a layer of mud that can be as thin as a protective cover or as thick as a mud wall. In simple houses the interior of the structural frame may be exposed. However, the interior is usually treated in some way: 1) with straw mats covering part of the wall or wall and ceiling; 2) with a mud surface on the walls and straw mats on the ceilings (in rectangular-plan houses); 3) with mud on both walls and ceiling creating an effect of vaulting (in round-plan houses). In all cases the intention is to keep the inner space cool and ventilated. When the houses are surfaced with a non-porous material like mud they are ventilated by an unsurfaced space between wall and roof, or by ventilation holes in the mud or straw wall when the structure is bare, or by ventilation devices on top of the doors, such as latticed upper panels. Floors are usually of packed dirt mixed with dung, regularly made wet to maintain a cool atmosphere. In az-Zuhra the floors are usually made of dried, sometimes patterned, mud. The houses may be part of a private compound, enclosed by walls of reed and twigs, mud or even brick. A compound which can easily be extended contains one or more sleeping huts, an outdoor cooking place (mud stove or oven, called *mawfan*) usually shaded, an enclosure for bath/toilet, a space for the storage of agricultural or fishing implements, an animal enclosure, and a shaded place for sitting and chewing *qat*. Some have a well. The compound can be easily extended.

Houses that are not part of a compound may still share communal facilities for cooking, sitting and chewing *qat* — generally outdoor activities. The main piece of furniture is the traditional bed or chair, a wooden frame about 70 x 170 cm. with a rope base 70 cm. above the ground.

*Top and Bottom:* Reed houses in ath-Thiyaby. The door sills and interiors are surfaced with mud textured with designs which the women imprint by hand when the clay is soft.

*(Opposite) Top and Right, in order from Left to Right:* Schematic sections of reed houses in al-Hudayda, al-Luhayya, al-Khawkha, Bajil, ᶜAbs and az-Zuhra. *Upper Centre, Lower Centre and Bottom Left, in order:* Compound walls near ᶜAbs, in al-Mansuriy and in al-Mukha.

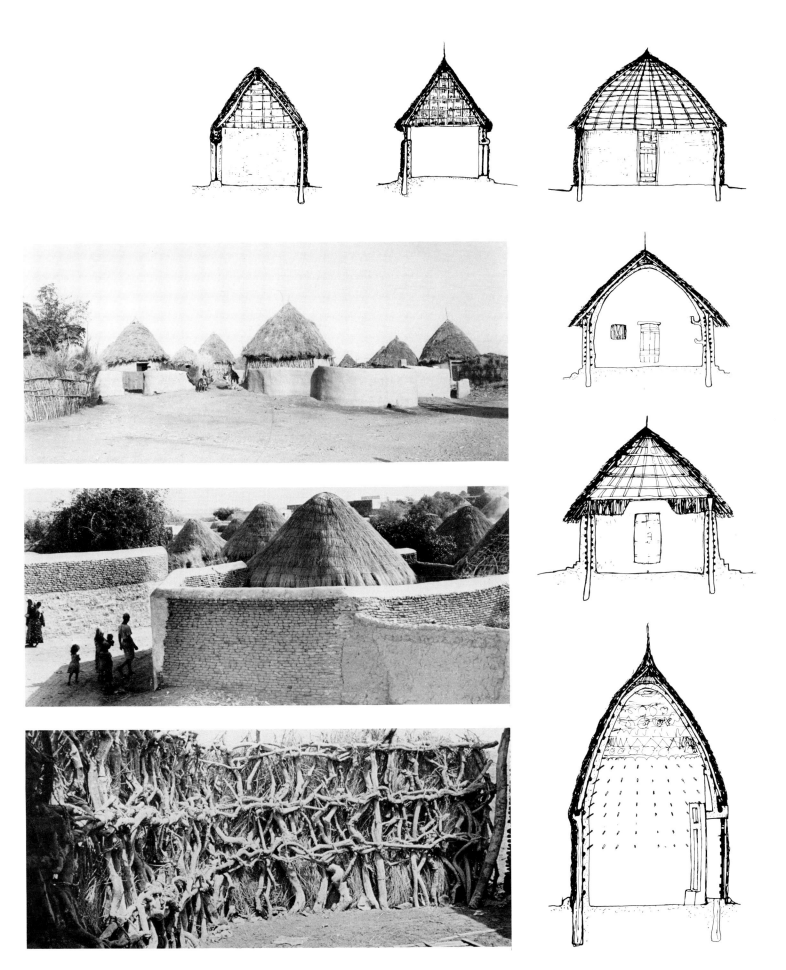

Throughout Tihama buildings are richly decorated. House decoration, often the responsibility of women, bears the mark of local traditions and inspiration. Decoration may have a functional aspect, like the ropes in geometric designs, or be purely aesthetic, such as the reliefs on the exterior or interior of mud walls, painted ceilings, or the arrangement of colourful enamel plates over large walls as is customary in much of northern Tihama. *Below:* Al-Luhayya. *(Opposite):* Az-Zuhra.

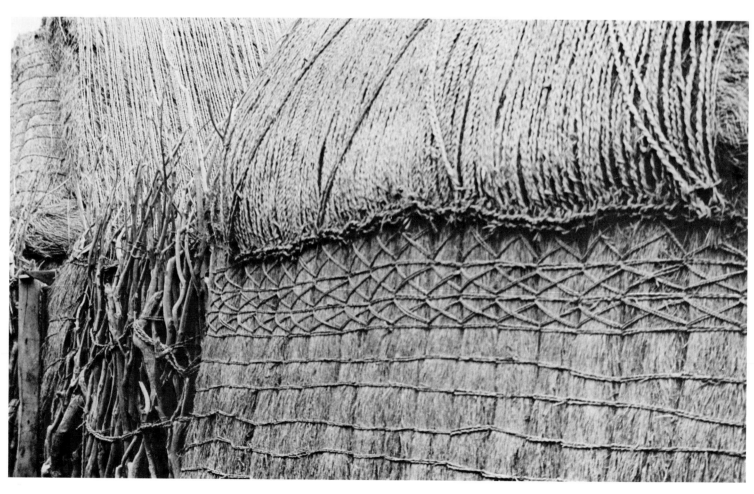

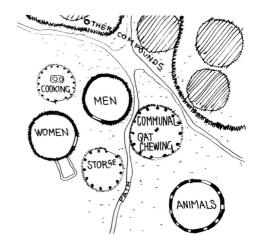

Az-Zuhra is the largest reed settlement where the treatment of both reed texturing and interiors is most refined. The houses are wide and lofty (they can be 6 m. in diameter with the interior more than 6 m. high) and organised in compounds. In front of each house a round area paved in dry mud and dung defines an intermediate zone between the communal area of the compound and the private space of the house. Inside the compound are three zones defined by enclosures made of light twigs and grass: one exclusive to the man, the chief of the family, one exclusive to women (where small children usually stay) and a common zone where one of the huts, usually a store, may also be a spare room for guests. The floors of these houses are made of mud with circular patterns similar to designs found in Africa. The interiors are completely surfaced in mud with a domed effect and fully decorated with paintings, often done by women, and enamel plates hanging from wood pegs embedded in the walls during construction. New themes often derive from the Civil War: planes, tanks and machine guns alongside cars, boats, hurricane lamps or waterpipes, all framed by stylised floral elements.

## FOREWORD CORRECTIONS

*Top of third column:*

When a top storey of mud is built over lower storeys of stone, the house style is defined by the stonework. On the other hand, when there are several mud floors above a stone section one or two storeys high, it is the former that determine the building style.

## OTHER CORRECTIONS AND OMISSIONS

*Page 82 — last two lines:*

and later in the house types adopted in the segregated Jewish neighbourhoods.

*Page 279 — 2nd column:*

caption *'Bottom'* refers to the opposite page (278).

## GLOSSARY CORRECTIONS

Refer to the main text for standard transliterations of Arabic terms.

| | |
|---|---|
| *barud* | shaded area outside, in coastal reed houses |
| *himyari* | referring to pre-Islamic kingdoms; popularly used to designate adapted or fully man-made caves |
| *mafraj al istiqbal* | should read *ghurfa al istiqbal* |
| *mafraj al majmu'a* | should read *ghurfa al majmu'a* |
| *malaj* | mud and dung sub-surfacing for ceilings and walls |
| *mawfan* | outdoor mud stove in coastal houses |
| *muqassis* | plasterer, white-washer |
| *muwaqqis* | stone cutter |
| *nawba* | watch tower |
| *qishr* | coffee husk, brewed as a hot drink |
| *saqf* | roof |
| *saqif* | stone temporary shelters |
| *shamsiya* | light well |

Page 141 *Top Left*

Page 156 *Top Right*

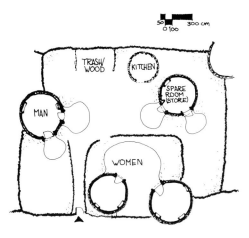

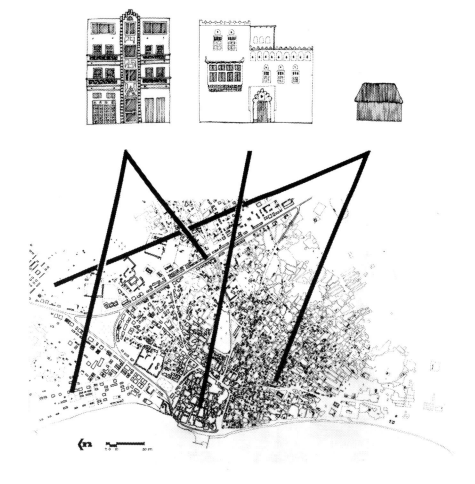

Page 281 *Top*

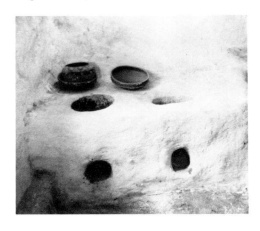

## FOREWORD CORRECTIONS

*Top of third column:*

When a top storey of mud is built over lower storeys of stone, the house style is defined by the stonework. On the other hand, when there are several mud floors above a stone section one or two storeys high, it is the former that determine the building style.

## OTHER CORRECTIONS AND OMISSIONS

*Page 82 — last two lines:*

and later in the house types adopted in the segregated Jewish neighbourhoods.

*Page 279 — 2nd column:*

caption 'Bottom' refers to the opposite page (278).

## GLOSSARY CORRECTIONS

Refer to the main text for standard transliterations of Arabic terms.

| | |
|---|---|
| *barud* | shaded area outside, in coastal reed houses |
| *himyari* | referring to pre-Islamic kingdoms; popularly used to designate adapted or fully man-made caves |
| *mafraj al istiqbal* | should read *ghurfa al istiqbal* |
| *mafraj al majmu'a* | should read *ghurfa al majmu'a* |
| *malaj* | mud and dung sub-surfacing for ceilings and walls |
| *mawfan* | outdoor mud stove in coastal houses |
| *muqassis* | plasterer, white-washer |
| *muwaqqis* | stone cutter |
| *nawba* | watch tower |
| *qishr* | coffee husk, brewed as a hot drink |
| *saqf* | roof |
| *saqif* | stone temporary shelters |
| *shamsiya* | light well |

Page 141 *Top Left*

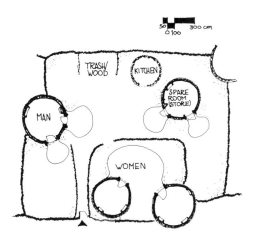

Page 281 *Top*

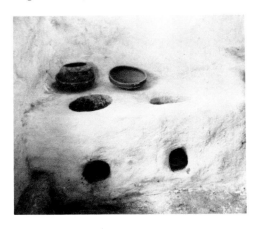

Page 156 *Top Right*

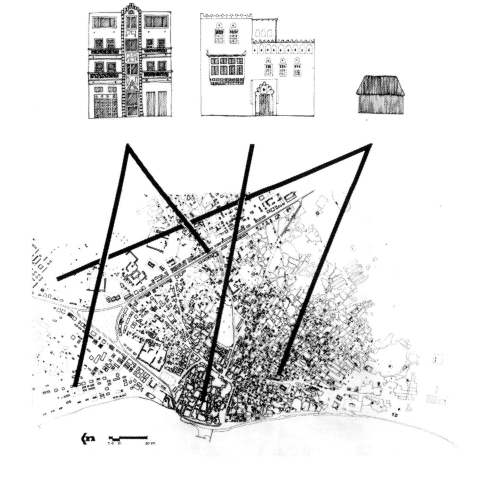

*Top Left:* Diagrammatic plan of compound, az-Zuhra. *Top Right and Bottom:* Reed house and compound, az-Zuhra.

*(Opposite) Top Left:* Diagrammatic plan of a house cluster in an 'open settlement', i.e. without compounds. *Top Right and Bottom:* ᶜAbs.

*Top and Bottom:* Painted ceiling and wall of a house in az-Zuhra.

*Top Right and Left:* Details of ceiling and wall pegs. *Centre Right and Left:* Door and interior. *Bottom:* Detail of mud floor.

The ruins of many Red Sea houses in al-Luhayya testify to the importance of this port between the 15th and early 19th centuries. These houses contain delicate wood carvings and painted ceilings (some still in good condition); the quality of their architecture is probably superior to al-Hudayda. In al-Luhayya today fishermen have developed a particular form of reed house, rectangular in plan, with original methods for weaving and ventilation. The houses are often topped by a crest. A shaded area (*barud,* 'cool place') for sitting and chewing *qat* also functions as a reception area outside the hut proper.

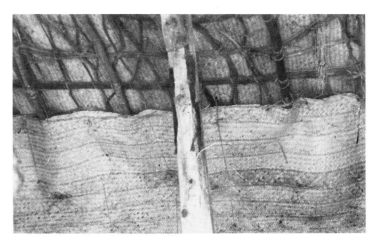

The *barud* may have the form of a Turkish ground-floor *diwan* common in the Red Sea houses and in San'a'. Interior walls and ceilings are surfaced with straw mats or the walls may be plastered using 'Turkish' decorative devices. *Top:* Al-Luhayya. Note the mosque on the left. *Centre Right:* Windows of 'Turkish' influence; white-plastered interior. *Centre Left: Barud;* interior. *Bottom Right:* Floor plans of two houses.

(*Opposite*) *Centre Right:* Ruins of Red Sea house. *Centre and Bottom Left:* Reed houses with characteristic roof crest.

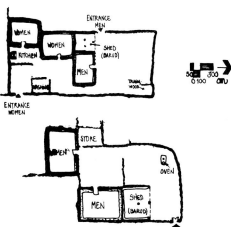

# 5. THE COASTAL STRIP

The Tihama brick house occurs in compounds not unlike the reed house compound. One-roomed structures in the form of rectangular prisms are built along the compound walls, which are at least 3 m. high and extend along the narrow streets. The decorative possibilities of brick are fully explored in the treatment of facades, friezes and cornices. Brick houses are most common in southern Tihama, in and around the city of Zabid. In northern Tihama these houses exist in the triangle roughly defined by ad-Dahi, al-Qanawis and az-Zaydiya, the last being the most important centre of brick architecture. Recently this type of building has been appearing in a simpler form, even in areas where reed building has been exclusive (for example, az-Zuhra), one reason being the higher status attributed to brick. *Top:* Walls of layered brick and river pebbles, Hays. *Bottom:* Reed and brick houses, al-Jarrahi.

*(Opposite) Top:* Brick surfaces in at-Tuhayta; *Bottom:* Brick surfaces near al-Qanawis.

146

## 5. THE COASTAL STRIP

Brick houses are usually one-storey structures, though houses with two storeys may be found in the larger cities. The basic spaces are a sleeping/reception room, an open roofed structure *(sfaf)* for sitting and chewing *qat* which doubles as a sleeping area on very hot nights, and a service area with several components like the reed house: kitchen, toilets, an animal enclosure and storage space. The entrance is frequently through a covered hall furnished with fixed benches and wooden Tihama chairs. *Top Right:* Axonometric of a brick house in Hays, the top room reached by an external stair being an independent dwelling unit. *Key:* 1. entrance hall; 2. reception room (men); 3. rooms (women); 4. *sfaf;* 5. spare room; 6. kitchen; 7 & 8. storage with room above; 9 & 10. terrace, WC; 11. animals; 12. access to adjoining compound. *Centre and Bottom:* Compound and *sfaf* in the same house.

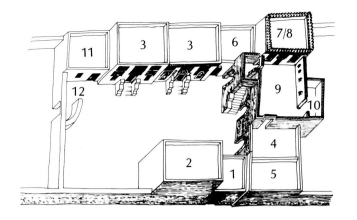

Below: Plans of a large two-storey brick house in Zabid. The house has an interior stair and the top rooms have access to the roof terrace. Top Left: External view of another house of the same type. Bottom Left: Entrance door. The decorative motifs are identical with those on Zabid's great mosque. Doors may be carved, often in the Indian style, and embellished with plaster carvings which contrast with the plain brick walls.

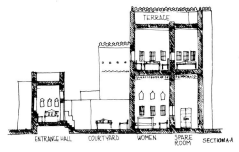

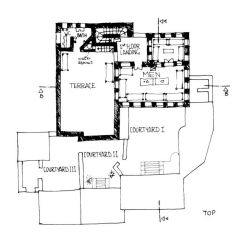

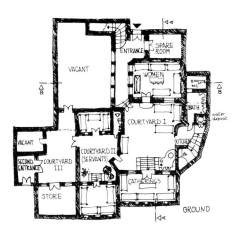

149

The facades facing the interior court-yards are covered with bas-reliefs in lime plaster made over a basic design in brick. In some areas the brick design is left exposed (ad-Dahi), or covered with a light plaster-layer (Zabid). Elsewhere designs are carved onto the plaster base (al-Mansuriya, Hays). This technique is still practised, though carvings may sometimes be made in cement with cruder results. *Top Left:* Drawing of a compound, Zabid. The enclosures in the foreground are bathrooms and water-storage areas. *Top Right and Bottom:* Zabid.
  *(Opposite)* Al-Mansuriya.

Ad-Dahi, beside Wadi Surdud in northern Tihama, contains some brick buildings though reed predominates. The refined brick work here, as in az-Zaydiya and al-Qanawis, is usually left exposed instead of being plastered over as in the south. *Top and Bottom:* Interior facade of main sleeping/reception room and entrance hall of the sheikh's house, ad-Dahi. The brick designs in the hall are underlined in light plaster and the name of Allah, written with eight bricks, is repeated around the walls.

The interiors of sleeping/reception rooms are elaborately carved with shelves and niches and decorated with other ornaments from enamel plates to Indian lithographs. Ceilings are frequently painted. The most refined examples of ceiling painting are found in the Red Sea houses, but the tradition is still maintained with the same basic patterns and enamel paint in modern building. *Top*

*Right and Left:* Textured ceilings in at-Tuhayta and Zabid. *Centre Right and Left:* Interiors in ad-Dahi and Zabid.

*(Overleaf) Top and Bottom:* Painted ceilings in Bayt al-Faqih and ad-Dahi. The chair repeats a similar pattern and colour scheme.

*(Opposite) Top and Bottom:* Modern interiors in az-Zaydiya and Zabid.

# 5. THE COASTAL STRIP

Concrete and cement blocks were introduced in the 1960s. Al-Hudayda, the provincial capital, is the best example of the use of these materials. Once a fisherman's town, then an important harbour (with al-Mukha and al-Luhayya), al-Hudayda prospered under the Turks but began to stagnate at the end of the last century. Since the Republican Revolution the town has once again expanded. The old central core consists of Red Sea architecture (represented elsewhere by al-Mukha and al-Luhayya). The new city of concrete constructions is supplanting the Red Sea core and pushing the reed constructions of the fishermen out to the fringes of the city. *Top Right:* Distribution of house types in al-Hudayda. *Bottom:* Typical reed house in al-Hudayda. A straw mat frames the door.

*(Opposite) Top:* Post-Revolution buildings. *Bottom:* General view of al-Hudayda.

157

## 5. THE COASTAL STRIP

Red Sea houses are town houses, usually of three or four storeys, built in coral-rock and/or brick, with an internal stair. Spatial organisation is hierarchical, as in the mountain house. The ground floor maybe a shop or warehouse, the main room on the next floor is a *diwan*; above is the sitting room *(majlis, diwan* or *mafraj).* A roof terrace *(kharja)* next to a covered area *(dharwa)* is typical, as is the wooden balcony *(rawshan* — now more commonly called *taqa).* Decorative treatment is concentrated in the carving of timber windows, doors and lintels. Brick reliefs and limestone carvings occur on cornice friezes and under windows. *Bottom Right:* Turkish window above porch leading to interior courtyard in the 'old town', al-Hudayda. *Bottom Left:* Street and mosque in the 'old town'.

*Top Left:* A fine Red Sea house with three *rawshan* and a dome (rare in secular architecture). The terrace is partly covered with a light zinc roof (in other cases a reed hut provides shade). *Bottom Left:* The ground floor of this Red Sea house was once a warehouse: note wooden balconies and canopies. *Centre Right:* Red Sea house with *rawshan*, wooden canopies, latticed windows, friezes and perforated arched parapets. The makeshift hut in the foreground is now a common sight.

# 5. THE COASTAL STRIP

Bottom Left: Detail of Red Sea house facade with carvings, latticed windows; Turkish balcony and brick and plaster screens enclosing the sleeping terrace (kharja). Right: Section and plans of Red Sea house near the suq.

(Opposite): Aspects of the same house. Top Right: Wooden ceiling of porch next to first-floor patio. Top Left: Wooden stair from first to second floor terraces. Centre: Wall carvings in majlis. Bottom: Majlis and Turkish window.

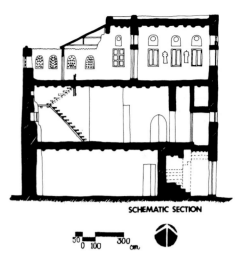

SCHEMATIC SECTION

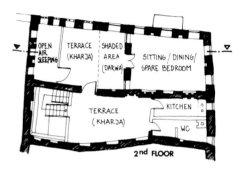

2nd FLOOR

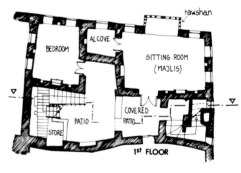

1st FLOOR

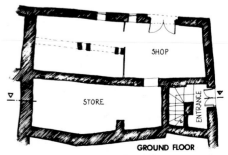

GROUND FLOOR

*Top, Right and Bottom:* Turkish windows. *Top Left:* Canopied balcony.

*(Opposite)* Decorative carvings on doors and on the ornate brackets projecting from the top corners of the door frame. The workmanship displays Indian influence. (Until the beginning of this century large numbers of Indian craftsmen and traders lived on the Yemeni coast.)

# 6. MIDLANDS AND HIGHLANDS

Stone architecture is predominant in the Midlands and the central spine of the Highlands, while pockets of mud or mud and stone architecture occur in the valleys and flatlands. Regional variation is found in the quality of stone and face cutting, wall ornamentation (inlaid or painted), and the importance of fenestration. Typological variations are generally irrelevant in defining regional characteristics. The following examples of stone architecture trace a course from north to south, and include, for reasons of geographic coherence, a few cases of mud architecture in areas where stone predominates. *Below:* View of al-Mahabisha, on the north-western edge of the Highlands.

## 6. MIDLANDS AND HIGHLANDS

*Below:* Major regional variations in stone architecture in the Midlands and Highlands. Regional styles are indicated by logos. The names refer either to a major settlement where a style is best represented or to a wider region with a fairly homogeneous style. *Top Right:* Transitional house type with stone walls and thatched roof, near Bajil, Tihama.

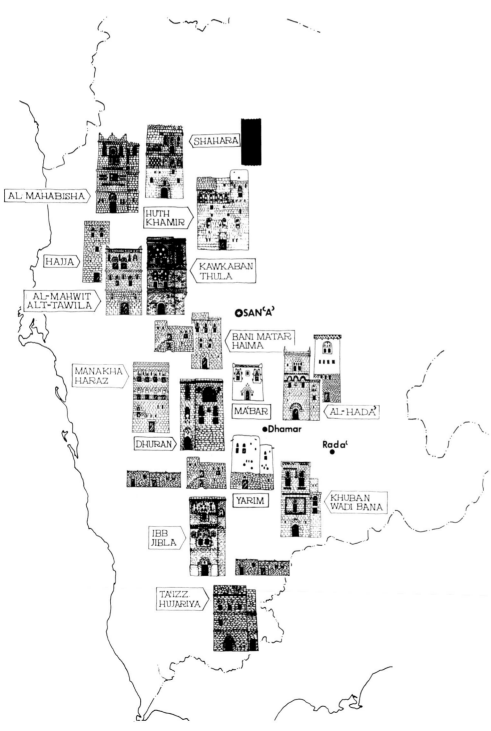

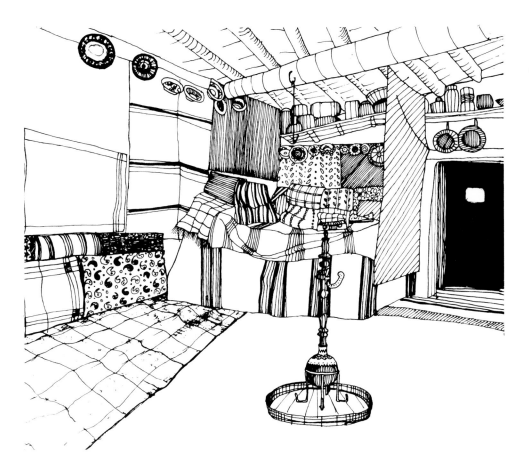

At the foothills bordering Tihama, stone walled huts with thatched roofs are isolated or grouped in small hamlets. Tihama influences are visible in the manner of dress (conical or wide-brimmed straw hats and often sleeveless white jackets) and in house furniture (the Tihama bed with colourful rugs and cushions co-exists with the floor mattress found all over the mountains). Window fanlights may have an opening wicket set in the *takhrim* for additional ventilation. Stone friezes are usually simple, contrasting with whitewash patterns on the walls and carved wood gratings in windows.

Al-Mahabisha is one of a string of towns strategically located on the mountains facing northern Tihama and similar in style to Washbah, the main town north of it. *Top Left:* House interior (from a photograph) displaying both mountain and Tihama furnishings, al-Mahabisha. Enamel plates on the walls are an additional decorative feature. *Bottom Right:* Wood gratings and simple friezes, al-Mahabisha. *Bottom Left:* Stone friezes and painted walls, al-Mahabisha. The fanlight has a wicket topped by a simple *takhrim*.

Shahara is an ancient royal town accessible only by winding paths negotiated by foot. It contains several examples of monumental architecture — a great mosque, the houses of the Imams and a slender bridge over a chasm separating the main settlement from a subsidiary one. The impregnability of the site made it an ideal headquarters for the Imams in their resistance against the Turks and later against the Republicans. However, the town was vulnerable to air raids and today it shows many scars from the Civil War. The architecture is austere. There are no *takhrim,* the upper windows having round or cruciform openings characteristic of archaic stone building, also seen in the Ibb-Jibla area in the southern Central Region. *Top Left:* Sharaha from a distance. *Bottom:* The severe architecture has no external ornamentation.

Characteristic elements of facade texturing are dented friezes, and round and cruciform openings for the upper window (now filled with rubble and small stones where previously small panes of alabaster let in additional light). The two square openings of the entrance door tympanum are typical of archaic stone building. White plaster splashed around the windows is common here as elsewhere. Several reasons for this have been suggested: as insect protection; to make the daylight appear brighter; or an easy way to 'decorate' the facade from within, not requiring scaffolding.

*Top Right:* Stone house with mud top floor, Khamir. *Bottom:* Large house in Huth. The large window of the top floor, a later addition, is in the San<sup>c</sup>a' style. Compare this with the windows below which have several openings in a darker stone frame.

Huth and Khamir are at both edges of a barren white rock plain which is dotted with watch towers. Huth is a market town while Khamir, on a small hill 12 km. south of Huth, is the seat of the most powerful confederation of tribes. The architecture of this area (which extends east to Dhi Bin and south to Raydah) is distinctive. The tall buildings of well-cut, almost white, limestone have small windows and fanlights reduced to square or round openings in an arched recess of the stone wall.

These, together with the sober stone reliefs, are often the only decorative elements in the facade. Additional ornamentation may be provided by whitewash patterns on the walls, in a bolder style than that of al-Mahabisha, or by black lava or basalt designs in horizontal stripes or around openings. Recent buildings usually have one or both forms of ornamentation. The top floor, in Khamir particularly, may be of mud. Interiors are severe, the dimly lit rooms only occasionally

brightened by *takhrim* instead of alabaster in the fanlights. Rooms may be plastered with gypsum or mud *(malaj)*. *Below and Bottom Left:* Roof terrace, plans and staircase of Khamir house. The roof terrace has an ablution place *(masfa)*. Personal rooms have their own bathroom (which is rare). The staircase is built with mud steps over a wooden structure. *Bottom Right:* Recent building in Khamir with painted and blackstone-inlay decorations.

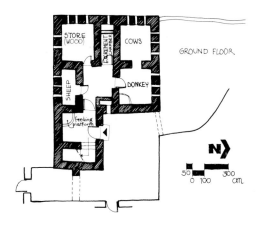

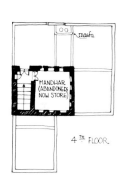

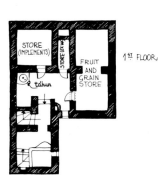

171

South-west of Khamir is Hajja. Nestled between two mountain peaks, Hajja had strategic importance. A fort-citadel was built by the Turks on the higher peak, and Turkish-style woodwork and balconies are found in the government building (*hukuma*) in the town centre. The wall textures, wall reliefs and friezes, and fenestration are common in mountain architecture, but some of the bold whitewashed or black designs covering the stone walls are unique. *Top Left:* Market street. *Centre Right:* Detail of house facade. *Bottom:* View towards the fort.

Al-Mahwit is a market town south of Hajja. The market place is located on a flat area on the edge of the town which stretches up the hill. On the hilltop the settlement is more dense and visibly older, containing examples of an architecture that has its fullest expression in Thula. The hillside houses have larger windows with fanlights made of one or two plates of alabaster joined vertically with plaster. Window sills are low, almost at floor level, and patterned fabric, rugs and cushions give rich colour to the interiors. Like at-Tawila, the architecture of al-Mahwit is ornamented with delicate friezes and inlays; rows or panels of square stones make variations on the same diamond-shaped theme. *Centre Left:* Market street. *Bottom:* The town. The market is in the foreground.

# 6. MIDLANDS AND HIGHLANDS

Main view, *mafraj* and plans of a hill-side house, al-Mahwit. Note the separate 'mother's kitchen' on the ground floor, used by the oldest woman in several large and wealthy families surveyed, and the central corridor, an elongation of the central distribution hall *(sa'la)*. The *hijra*, as a semi-private ante-chamber for one or two rooms, is also found in al-Mahwit/at-Tawila architecture.

*(Opposite) Top:* Characteristic stone patterns around windows and friezes. *Bottom Right:* Hilltop building similar to the Thula style. *Bottom Left:* Facade of house described above.

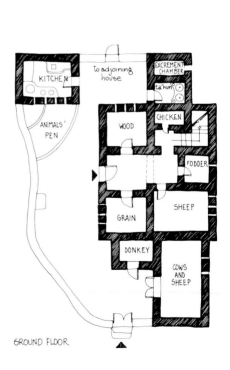

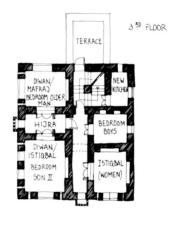

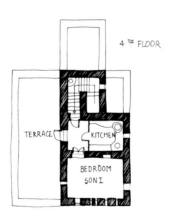

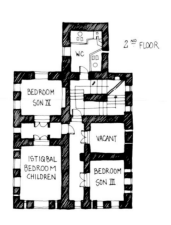

174

## 6. MIDLANDS AND HIGHLANDS

Less than one day's walk from al-Mahwit, and framed by majestic scenery, is at-Tawila. This town is remarkable not only because of its stone treatment, but also because of its tradition of *takhrim* designs and colours. Most houses display two narrow *takhrim* on both sides of the windows. The market, dominated by the Great Mosque, is an important centre in the Highlands. *Top Right:* At-Tawila, at the foot of a steep hill. *Bottom:* Facades are characterised by stone work in friezes and around openings, *takhrim* and vertical loop holes flanking windows.

*Left:* Street in at-Tawila. *Above:* House interior. Note the *takhrim* on both sides of the main window.

*(Opposite) Top:* Detail of town wall with building on top. *Bottom:* Kawkaban deserted.

Half-a-day's walk to the west, on the edge of a steep cliff overlooking Shibam al-Aqyan, lies Kawkaban. Once the capital of an ancient kingdom and a site of pre-Islamic culture, Kawkaban had an impregnable position; like Shahara, Civil War air attacks left it in ruins. The archi-

tecture is austere in spite of a profusion of inlaid stone designs. Houses are of high quality with frequent top courts and central light-wells. *Top, Centre Left and Bottom Left:* Stone inlay work in Kawkaban is similar to that found in Thula, but more restrained. *Centre Right and Bottom Right:* Section and lightwell of a house with a top court.

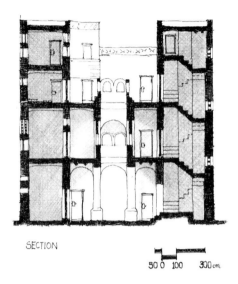

SECTION

50 0  100    300 cm

# 6. MIDLANDS AND HIGHLANDS

Thula, on the plain below Kawkaban, is a walled city at the foot of a fortified rock pinnacle. It has always been a free town, independent of vassalage to the various lords who have dominated the region. It contains the most sophisticated examples of flag-stone treatment and striking urban ambiances created by paved streets and high, finely textured walls. Houses with top courts and lightwells are common. The market is comparably small. *Top:* Town walls joining the fortified pinnacle, Thula. *Bottom:* Thula street.

*(Opposite)* Thula building.

*This page:* Friezes and wall textures, Thula.

*(Opposite)* External view, sections, plans and distribution hall lightwell of a large house with top court and several lightwells, Thula.

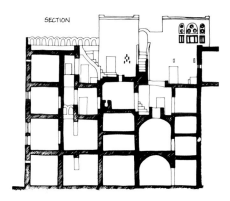

SECTION

3 RD FLOOR

STORE / FARM TOOLS | TA'HUN | GRAIN STORE | WC
ROOM | LIGHT WELL | STORE WOOD | STORE
GRAIN STORE | SHEEP | GRAIN STORE

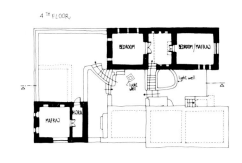

4 TH FLOOR

BEDROOM | BEDROOM / MAFRAJ
light well
MAFRAJ | HIJRA

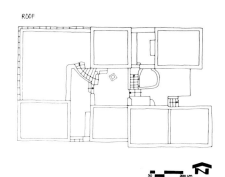

ROOF

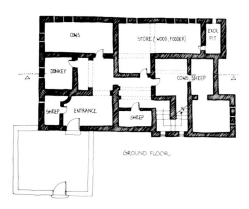

GROUND FLOOR

COWS | STORE (WOOD, FODDER) | EXCR PIT
DONKEY | COWS, SHEEP
SHEEP | ENTRANCE | SHEEP

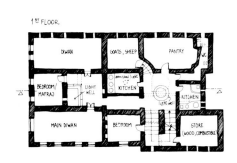

1 ST FLOOR

DIWAN | GOATS, SHEEP | PANTRY | WC
BEDROOM / MAFRAJ | LIGHT WELL | KITCHEN | KITCHEN
MAIN DIWAN | BEDROOM | STORE (WOOD, COMBUSTIBLE)

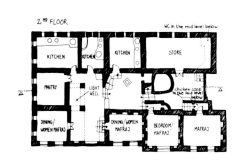

2 ND FLOOR

WC in the mud level below
KITCHEN | KITCHEN | KITCHEN | STORE
PANTRY | LIGHT WELL | chicken coop in the mud level below
DINING / WOMEN MAFRAJ | DINING / WOMEN MAFRAJ | BEDROOM / MAFRAJ | MAFRAJ

50 0 100 300 cm

183

# 6. MIDLANDS AND HIGHLANDS

The regions of Bani Matar and al-Hayma are west of San'a', before the Haraz chain of mountains is reached. Tower houses in this area are texturally simple, the main decorative element consisting of outlining with white plaster the joints around openings. There are many examples of two-storey houses with external stairs, and a variation with closed ground-level courts, sometimes completely covered, and a stair to one or two rooms on top. Al-Hayma is scenically dramatic with its terraced slopes descending to deep *wadis* dotted with small clusters of tall tower houses, while Bani Matar,

with Yemen's highest mountain, Jabal an-Nabiy Shu'ayb, has a just claim to glory. *Below Left:* The walled village of Bayt Na'ama, Bani Matar. *Centre Left:* White plaster window decorations in al-Yazil, Bani Matar. *Right Side and Bottom:* Section, plans and interior of house with covered distribution court *(sa'la)* off the market, Kkamis al-Madyur, al-Hayma.

*(Opposite) Top and Bottom Right:* Bayt Mahdam, Bani Matar. *Top and Centre Left:* Section and plan of top floor of a house with a covered entrance court, Bayt Mahdam, Bani Matar. *Bottom Left:* Khamis al-Madyur, al-Hayma.

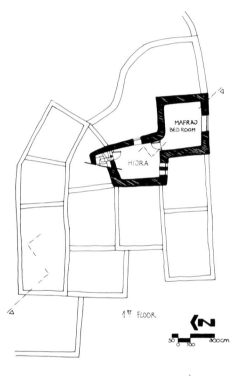

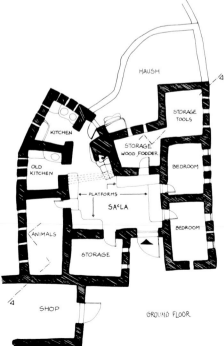

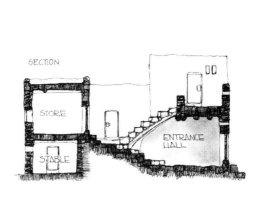

SECTION

STORE

STABLE

ENTRANCE HALL

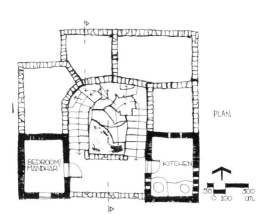

PLAN

BEDROOM/ MANDHAR

KITCHEN

50    300
0  100    cm

185

# 6. MIDLANDS AND HIGHLANDS

The last high mountains between Sanᶜa' and al-Hudayda are those of Haraz, once the stronghold of the Ismaili sect of Islam. Manakha, the main market town of this sub-region, is imposingly located on one of the peaks a little apart from al-Hajra, a village which used to be the market site on the old Sanᶜa'-al-Hudayda road. Patterned wall painting with flamboyant designs exists in this region, though less sophisticated than examples already illustrated. Window fanlights are frequently made of a single alabaster circle, and display on the outside a metal lattice screen unique to the region. *Top Right:* Street in Manakha. Note the screens protecting the fanlights. *Bottom:* Al-Hajra.

*(Opposite) Top Left:* Sheikh's house, al-Hajra. *Top Right, Centre and Bottom:* Interior, bathroom, hallway designs and section of a house, al-Hajra.

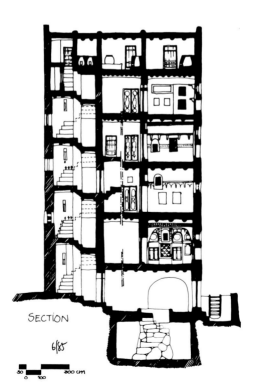

SECTION

6/85

187

Dawran, south of Haraz in the mountains of ᶜAnis, was for a time a royal town. The arches and inlaid brickwork on stone walls, as well as timber gratings, belong to the style of a wider area centred in Dhamar, the largest city on the plains to the south-east. The Great Mosque of Dawran is a twin construction to that of ar-Rawda, near Sanᶜa'. *Centre Right:* Detail of inlaid brickwork on stone wall. *Centre Left, Bottom Left and Right:* Facade, schematic plan and cistern *(ma'jil)* of a house within a compound, Dawran. Compounds of two or three houses belonging to the local aristocracy are seen in many provincial towns. The example here, now abandoned, is complete with its own cistern, warehouse *(samsara)* and large entrance court. The walls are high enough to be defensive. The main entrance is through an arched door above which is the guard house. On top of the entrance is the *mafraj.*

*(Opposite) Top:* Dawran. The market *(left)* and the mosque dome *(centre)* are visible. *Bottom:* Facades with characteristic double and triple fanlight openings for larger windows.

Key:
1. entrance and guard house;
2. main houses;
3. warehouse;
4. cistern;
5. entrance court;
6. wood and straw deposit (occasional guard post).

## 6. MIDLANDS AND HIGHLANDS

East of the ʿAnis mountains, a large central plateau between the western and eastern Highlands stretches from Maʿbar to Yarim. Maʿbar and its twin village, al-Wasta, are isolated instances of wholly mud building in an area of stone or mixed construction. These mud houses are not more than two storeys, with an internal stair and sanitary shafts creating interesting volumetric effects. These are open settlements without defined boundaries, structurally closer to the low mud houses of the Eastern Plateau than to mountain architecture. Decorations of inset triangular motifs made with mud blocks appear towards the east in al-Hada', the neighbouring mountains, and again in Dhamar, the main city of the plains. However, it is in Maʿbar that this simple decorative device gains most importance in the overall appearance of the house. Plastering around windows is also used for characteristic decorative effect. The main door is framed by an inverted stone trapeze inset in the mud wall. *Centre:* Al-Wasta. *Bottom:* House in Maʿbar.

*(Opposite) Top Right and Left:* Plans and stair of Maʿbar house on previous page. Note the separate one-storey building for the women's quarters. *Bottom: Mafraj.*

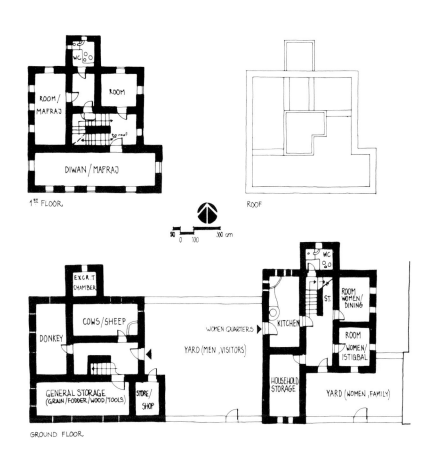

1ˢᵀ FLOOR

ROOF

| ROOM / MAFRAJ | ROOM |
| WC | |
| DIWAN / MAFRAJ | |

**GROUND FLOOR**

EXCR.T CHAMBER

DONKEY

COWS/SHEEP

GENERAL STORAGE (GRAIN/FODDER/WOOD/TOOLS)

STORE / SHOP

WOMEN QUARTERS

YARD (MEN, VISITORS)

WC

KITCHEN

ST.

ROOM WOMEN/ DINING

ROOM WOMEN/ ISTIGBAL

HOUSEHOLD STORAGE

YARD (WOMEN, FAMILY)

# 6. MIDLANDS AND HIGHLANDS

In the region of al-Hada' on the eastern fringes of the Highlands well-defined stone and mud architecture co-exists. The first two floors of mud buildings are always of stone: the mud construction above has affinities with the region of Khawlan in the north, with its projecting cornices or rooftops adorned by simple friezes of blocks in triangular designs. The decorative features of stone constructions are similar to those found in the eastern Highlands from al-Hada' to Wadi Bana. Alternations of light with dark stone and traditional inlays of rows of square stones are common. A constant motif which recurs throughout the eastern Highlands is the X-shaped stone inlaid in friezes and window sills. Houses with top court and lightwells are also found. This region contains important pre-Islamic remains; the tribes who live here retain strong ancestral ties with tribes in the area of Ma'rib, near the ancient capital of the kingdom of Saba'. *Below:* Mud and stone architecture in Qihlan. Note the mud-block friezes and the stone framed windows.

*Top Left:* Stable in al-Mithal. *Bottom:* A recent house in Bani ᶜAqrut, in which traditional elements (friezes of X-shaped stones, triangles, diamond inlays) are combined with urban decorative features found in Dhamar (alternating bands of two-coloured stone and the method of stone cutting).

## 6. MIDLANDS AND HIGHLANDS

View, *mafraj* and plans of sheikh's house, al-Mithal. This house consists of three independent housing blocks, internally connected, for the sheikh and his brothers, and functions as a 'fort citadel' when necessary. There are many light-wells for hallways and stairways.

*(Opposite) Top: Mafraj* wall with characteristic friezes and dark stone designs. The fanlights are made of small alabaster panes set into a stone frame. Note how the stone elements are cut. *Bottom Right: Lightwell. Bottom Left:* Stairway.

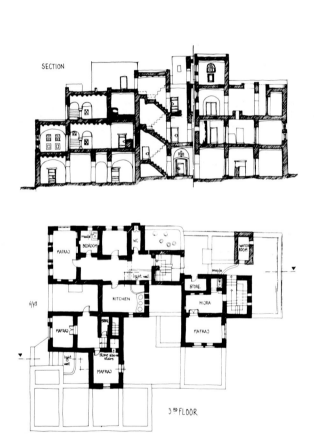

SECTION

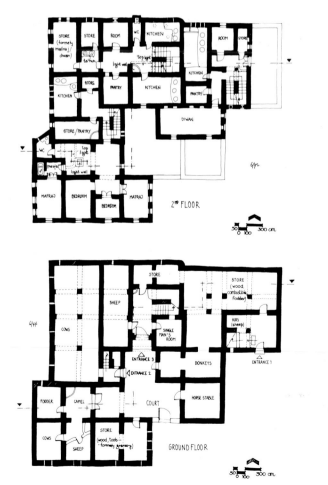

## 6. MIDLANDS AND HIGHLANDS

The transition between Al-Hada' and Khuban, further south, is made by the flatlands between the towns of Dhamar and Rada$^c$, speckled with small settlements with well-defined boundaries. The architecture is rural but shows some influence from the two nearby towns. Dhu Awlayin, set on a small elevation, is confined by an outer belt of houses. Numerous buildings bridge the streets, the succession of arches and galleries creating an enclosed atmosphere. *Top and Bottom:* Section, view and plans of a house in Dhu Awlayin with an external stair. *Centre:* Dhu Awlayin street.

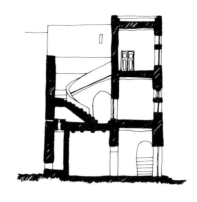

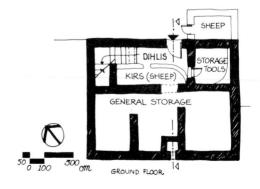

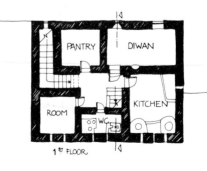

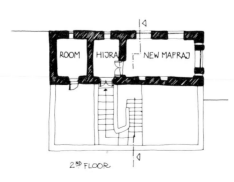

196

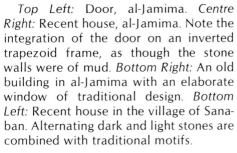

*Top Left:* Door, al-Jamima. *Centre Right:* Recent house, al-Jamima. Note the integration of the door on an inverted trapezoid frame, as though the stone walls were of mud. *Bottom Right:* An old building in al-Jamima with an elaborate window of traditional design. *Bottom Left:* Recent house in the village of Sanaban. Alternating dark and light stones are combined with traditional motifs.

# 6. MIDLANDS AND HIGHLANDS

The mountains of Khubban, south-east of Yarim, shelter many small settlements short distances apart; these vary from troglodyte dwellings to complex walled villages with collective services. The treatment of materials has many features in common with other regions already described — as part of a 'standard mountain style' — and especially with al-Hada[c]. South of this area is Wadi Bana, a fertile valley along which more sophisticated settlements are found. *Top Right:* Khubban landscape. *Centre:* Bayt Hilbub. *Bottom:* Mosque baths and pool, Dhi Ashra[c].

(*Opposite*) Facade of characteristic design and interior, al-Kitba.

## 6. MIDLANDS AND HIGHLANDS

Rural house featuring top light holes for hallways and kitchen, al-Mawra, Khubban. *Top Right:* Facade showing double fanlights on windows of main reception room. *Below:* Living/sleeping room, the walls adorned with graffiti by the women of the house. *Centre and Bottom:* Section and plans; top court and chimney.

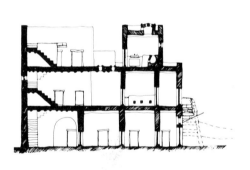

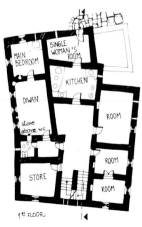

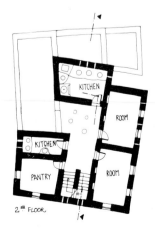

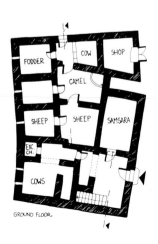

GROUND FLOOR.

1ST FLOOR.

2ND FLOOR.

*Top Right:* Large house displaying sophisticated stonework and fanlight fretwork, Sadda. The standard of construction in this market town overlooking a stream in Wadi Bana is generally high. *Bottom Right:* The new market — a long row of shops and warehouses suited to car traffic, Sadda. *Bottom Left:* New building, Sadda. The quality of traditional stone finishing is not matched by the new utilities. *Centre Right:* Facade in an-Nadira. The fanlights in the lower windows — two square openings topped by an arched opening — are typical of the oldest architecture in the region.

## 6. MIDLANDS AND HIGHLANDS

*This page:* Yarim lies at the southern end of the plateau near the ancient *himyaritic* capital, Dhafar. The construction here is a mixture of stone (the bottom floors) and mud (the top floors). Mud floors usually project a little over the stone infra-structure. The style is unornamented. The oldest examples have simple round alabaster fanlights with no external plastering; more recent buildings have an arched window simply framed by a plaster strip. Around Yarim are many two-storey houses, in both mud and stone, with an external stair.

*(Opposite)* Dumran, west of Yarim.

Ibb, a provincial capital in one of Yemen's most fertile areas, was originally a walled hilltop town which later spread into the valley. After the construction of the Sanʿaʾ-Taʿizz road, a new central market was built in this vicinity. An aqueduct brings water from the nearby mountains, though piped water is now replacing this system. The town displays many traditional features, from the ornamental vocabulary of sober stone friezes to fanlights with multiple alabaster panes set in a stone frame sometimes surfaced with lime plaster. The openings are normally round or arched, but they may also be cruciform as in Shahara. Lime plaster is commonly used for carvings with elementary designs as well as more sophisticated bas-reliefs with stylised floral elements or motifs derived from a small ball in a triangle or lozenge. Wall joints may be outlined with plaster. New constructions favour the use of orange-coloured lava stone brought 80 km. by lorry, instead of the grey- or pink-toned stone of the region. *Top:* Mountain view of Ibb. *Bottom Right and Left:* Street and part of the old stone-paved market in the town centre.

*(Opposite)* Tall buildings in narrow street.

## 6. MIDLANDS AND HIGHLANDS

A house over 300 years old. *Top and Centre:* Section and plans. *Bottom Right: Mafraj* on the top floor which doubles as a formal dining room and a sleeping room for the head of the family. *Bottom Left:* View from the street. Note the thick lime plaster footing and simple friezes.

*(Opposite) Top Right: Nura* reliefs on *mafraj* wall. *Top Left:* Entrance hall *(dihliz). Centre:* Plans. *Bottom right:* Bathroom and toilet on the first floor. *Bottom Left:* Family dining room.

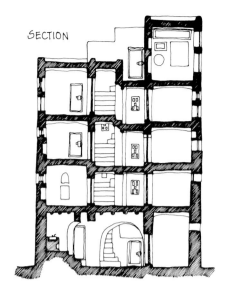

SECTION

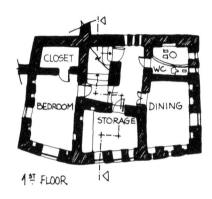

50 0 100 300 cm
N

GRANARY
WOOD FODDER
EXCR. PIT
ANIMALS
TAHUN
DIHLIS

GROUND FLOOR

CLOSET
WC
BEDROOM
STORAGE
DINING

1<sup>ST</sup> FLOOR

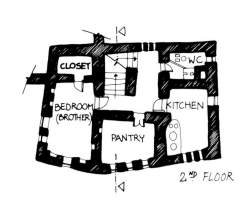

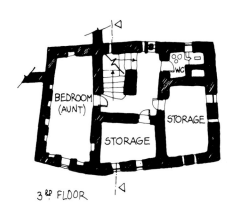

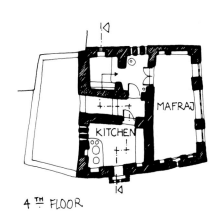

2ND FLOOR

3RD FLOOR

4TH FLOOR

Jibla, near Ibb, is historically the most important town in the Midlands. The architectural style is identical to that of Ibb, though more refined in details of ornamentation. A pink-toned stone is used which makes an attractive contrast with the green surroundings. *Top Right:* Brick minaret (detail). *Top Left:* Windows with lime plaster carvings. *Bottom:* General view.

*(Opposite)* Characteristic windows and doors with side benches thickly coated with lime plaster, Ibb.

# 6. MIDLANDS AND HIGHLANDS

At the foot of Jabal Sabr lies Taᶜizz, capital of al-Hujjariya province and at various times the capital of Yemen. Its golden period under the Rasulids (13th-15th centuries) left the town a most important monumental heritage, its mosques. After the Revolution the town expanded with concrete apartment buildings displaying violent combinations of colour on their painted facades. More recently, stone buildings have appeared in a wide variety of stone hewing and colours. The oldest part of the town is, like a large village, enlivened by an important though spatially simple market: one main street connects the two gates with secondary branches. *Top Right:* Domed tomb of a holy man *(wali)*. These are common in al-Hujjariya, as in Tihama, and are often popular pilgrimage sites. *Bottom:* View of Taᶜizz with post-Revolution buildings in the foreground and the 'old town' and its mosques behind.

*(Opposite) Top:* Aspects of the 'old town'. *Bottom:* House interior with characteristic arched niches and unusual wooden fretwork.

The architecture of al-Hujjariya is plain. Ornamentation consists of simple friezes and lime plaster work in the fanlight tympanum; joints are covered with mortar, except in the area of Jabal Sabr where buildings have dry stone walling. Here, the main external feature is the waste shaft terminating in arches at ground level giving access to the collecting chamber. In the area of Turba, windows frequently have wooden lattice shutters. Interior niches, both for fanlights and for storage, are usually arched, not rectangular as elsewhere. *Below:* Jabal Sabr.

*(Opposite)* Farmer's house with entrance courtyard and lightwell to hallway, Jabal Sabr. *Top:* Facade and general view. *Centre:* Plans and section (first floor, not represented, is identical to second floor and used for storage). *Bottom Right:* Blind arches in entrance courtyard wall. *Bottom Left:* Windows of second floor room *(al-istiqbal)* with timber lattice parapet.

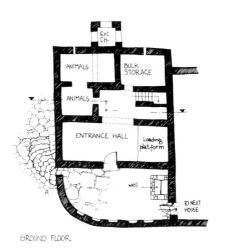

EXC. CH.

ANIMALS | BULK STORAGE

ANIMALS

ENTRANCE HALL | loading platform

well

TO NEXT HOUSE

GROUND FLOOR

WC

FAMILY GATHERINGS ROOM (ISTIQBAL) | STORE

top light

ROOM (father) | ROOM (son)

2ᴺᴰ FLOOR

50  100  300 cm
0

KITCHEN

light well

3ᴿᴰ FLOOR

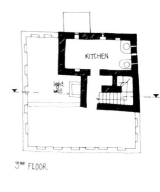

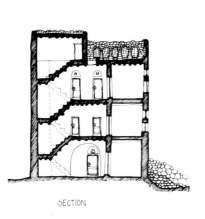

SECTION

*Top and Centre Right, and Left Column:* External view, view from roof terrace and floor plans of the house of a wealthy family in al-Jabbana, Turba. *Bottom Right:* Al-Jabbana. Note the prominent waste shaft on the centre building.

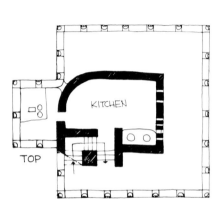

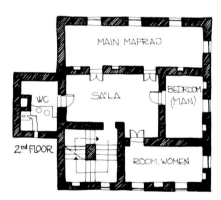

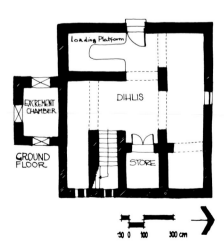

*Left:* Detail of facade with timber-latticed windows and lime plaster treatment in the border of the recessed fanlights. *Right:* Interior of a similar house, Turba.

# 7. EASTERN HIGHLANDS AND PLATEAU

Mud construction has already been noted in regions where stone predominates: in fact it is found in most of the country. However, mud gains complete architectural expression in the north and north-eastern fringes of the Highlands, the Eastern Plateau, and the semi-desert mountains of the south-east. Chapter four has already described the technology of mud building in its two basic forms: coursed clay (*zabur*) and sun-dried blocks (*libn*). To some degree, both methods are employed throughout, but in finished architectural form these may be regionally located. The north and north-east are the major areas for *zabur*, with local stylistic variations existing short distances apart. Towards the centre of the Highlands *libn* is popular, sometimes in combination with *zabur* on the lower floors. In the survey which follows, construction is entirely in mud except in the south-east where stone is used alongside and in combination with mud in characteristic styles.

*Above:* Saᶜda from the north.
*(Opposite)* Village in the Saᶜda region.

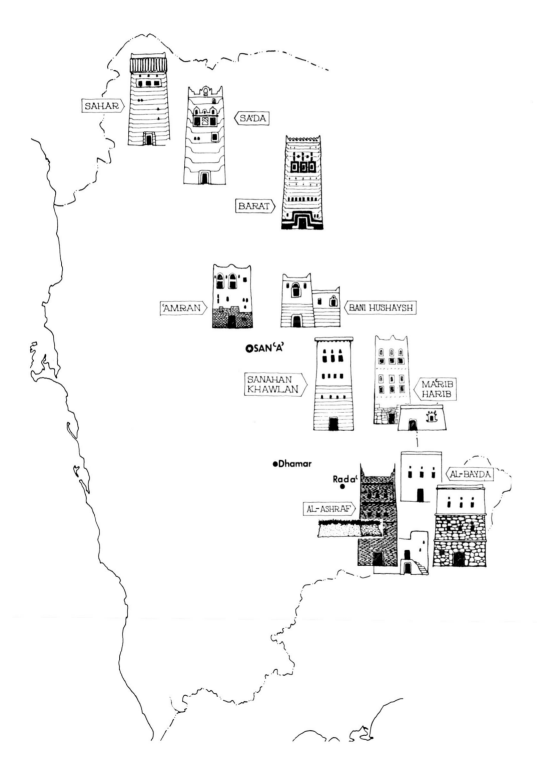

*Left:* Major regional variations in the northern and eastern Highlands, the Eastern Plateau, and the south-east. Regional styles are indicated by logos. Names refer either to major settlements where a style is best represented or to a wider region with a fairly homogenous style. In the south-east, logos refer to both mud and stone constructions.

*(Opposite) Top:* The landscape of Sahar. *Bottom:* The settlement of Saᶜda.

# 7. EASTERN HIGHLANDS AND PLATEAU

The area north of Saʿda consists of long flat stretches of semi-desert dotted with small thorny bushes, surrounded by barren mountains. Farming takes place in the narrow valleys at the foothills and in the plains. The main markets have permanent mud stalls, next to which temporary stalls may be set up in tents. Buildings in this region are made in *zabur,* with strongly marked separations between the layers: mud surfacing *(malaj)* is rarely seen. There are few decorative features other than a fluted band along the tops of the buildings (seen also in the Eastern Plateau). Top courts with lightwells are found in larger houses, suggesting a possible link with Saudi Arabian buildings to the north. *Centre:* Vineyards, Ta'la. *Bottom:* Mejis.

*(Opposite) Top Right:* Detail of pierced parapet surfaced with lime plaster from the sheikh's house, Ta'la. *Bottom:* This house has top courts, lightwells and a more elaborate decoration. The top floor of brick with a succession of simple friezes is a later addition. *Top Left:* Detail of facade.

## 7. EASTERN HIGHLANDS AND PLATEAU

Sa'da, the most important town in the north, is the first centre of the Zaydi Imams; according to a local tradition, however, the original settlement was at the foothills a short distance to the south. The architectural style of this walled town is unique, with a refined decorative treatment of *zabur* walls, sometimes coated with mud *(malaj)*. Roofs are usually topped with parapets of small arches plastered over with lime. Windows are decorated with lime designs: the oldest display fanlights with two or three round alabaster panes vertically disposed in a complex niche adorned with carvings. Rows of baked bricks are often used to 'finish' the top of a building in a simple frieze. The largest houses may be contained within an enclosure with two or more other constructions. In this case a reception room *(mafraj)* is usually built over the entrance area in addition to the main *mafraj* on the top floor. *Centre:* Vineyards surrounding Sa'da.

*(Opposite) Top:* The town wall. *Bottom:* Roof tops.

*Top:* Building surfaced with mud and enclosure wall. The clay courses on the wall are exposed. *Bottom Left:* Twin-towered building with a new metal door. The roof of the structure connecting the towers may function as an open court. *Bottom Right:* Bridged-over streets are part of the townscape.

*(Opposite) Top:* Decorative features may be sober, as here. *Bottom:* Other buildings display a variety of friezes, designs round openings and roof parapets.

*Top Left and Bottom:* External view and axonometric drawing of houses in a typical compound. *Top Right:* Detail of the oldest house in the compound. This has an intricate system of bridges, terraces and external stairs connecting with subsidiary buildings. The ablution place *(masfa)* adjoining the *mafraj* on the top floor is typical. The most recent and largest house has a brick top floor. Note the talismanic horns jutting out from the roof corners.

*(Opposite) Top Right and Left:* Fanlight niche of typical design and entrance patio. *Below:* Floor plans.

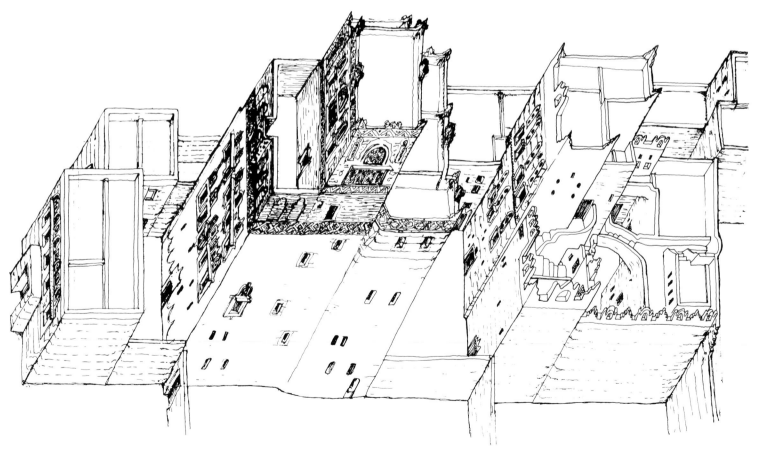

4ᵗʰ FLOOR

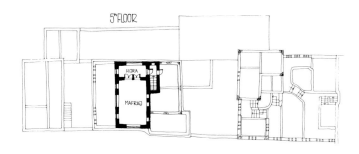

5ᵗʰ FLOOR

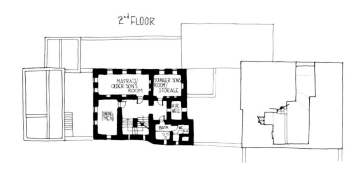

2ⁿᵈ FLOOR

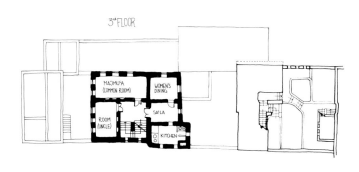

3ʳᵈ FLOOR

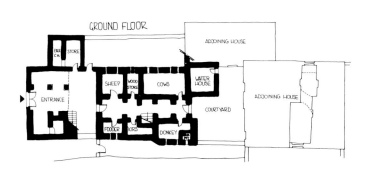

GROUND FLOOR

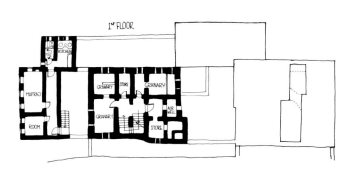

1ˢᵗ FLOOR

Sa'da, being on the main road to Saudi Arabia, has changed irrevocably since it was opened to vehicular traffic. In order to preserve the architectural integrity of the old town, a satellite town was planned for the vicinity but construction has continued to cling outside the town walls. Stone has become the prestigious new material, used for example in institutional buildings financed by foreign aid. *Centre Right and Left:* Facade of stone arches around a *zabur* building and a row of shops outside Bab al-Yaman, one of the main gates destroyed to allow vehicle access. *Bottom:* Town skyline.

*(Opposite) Mafraj* of the oldest house in the compound described on page 226.

# 7. EASTERN HIGHLANDS AND PLATEAU

*Zabur* is also the main method of construction in an area extending to the Eastern Plateau, from Barat to the Jawf. Here the material has a different texture and the architectural style is distinct, despite some similarity with other regions — such as the grooved band of mud along the top of buildings. Colour is the main decorative device, applied to interiors and exteriors in stripes of red ochre, alternating with bands of yellow ochre and white plaster around openings. Roofs are often topped by a row of white-plastered triangular motifs. *Below:* Suq al-ᶜIn'an, a market village surrounded by granite on a flat top in the Barat mountains. Though stone is readily available, all construction is in mud; this includes most mosques and minarets which elsewhere tend to be built in brick or stone in areas where mud is used.

*(Opposite)* Isolated villages in a *wadi* near the foot of the Barat mountain.

*(Overleaf) Top:* Grooved band topped by a row of triangular motifs. *Bottom:* The waste shaft is a dominant feature of Barat architecture. *(Opposite)* House interior and street, Suq al-ᶜInan.

Housing compound, Suq al-ᶜInan. The oldest house, circular in plan, is now closed. The building surveyed now houses the main branch of the family. *Top and Centre Right:* Entrance hall with red ochre stripes; door to the roof terrace. *Centre Left:* View of compound. *Bottom:* Floor plans. Note the WC on the top floor with access only from the terrace (hygenic prejudice). On the floor below are the main living/ sleeping rooms with an enclosed ablution place in the corner.

*(Opposite)* Buildings of a similar type. Note the plaster and stripes at lowest terrace.

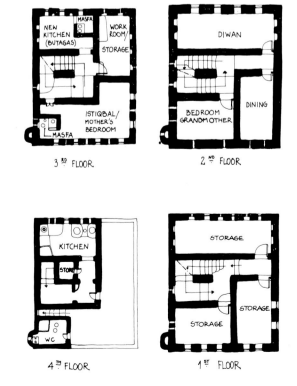

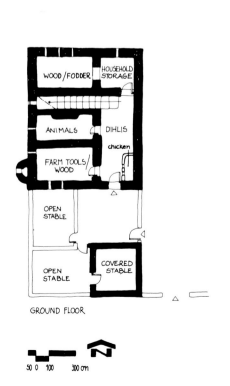

3 RD FLOOR.

NEW KITCHEN (BUTAGAS) — MASFA — WORK ROOM/ STORAGE — ISTIQBAL/ MOTHER'S BEDROOM — MASFA

2 ND FLOOR.

DIWAN — DINING — BEDROOM GRANDMOTHER

4 TH FLOOR.

KITCHEN — STORE — WC

1 ST FLOOR.

STORAGE — STORAGE — STORAGE

GROUND FLOOR

WOOD/FODDER — HOUSEHOLD STORAGE — ANIMALS — DIHLIS — chicken — FARM TOOLS/ WOOD — OPEN STABLE — OPEN STABLE — COVERED STABLE

50 0 100 300 cm

## 7. EASTERN HIGHLANDS AND PLATEAU

Khiràb, in the foothills, is similar in architectural style, though the buildings here have a more angular shape and the adornment of roofs with triangular motifs is more widespread. The architecture of Khirab also favours buttresses against walls or flanking the main doors. *Top Right:* Wall buttresses. *Bottom:* Market square.

*(Opposite)* Examples of wall texturing.

Harf, in the area of as-Sufyan, maintains the same basic style but without colour or decorative detail. The buildings here have a certain brutalism in their desolate surroundings.

Deeper into the Highlands, at the northern end of a valley stretching to Sanᶜa', lies the ancient stone-walled town of ᶜAmran. The town contains many pre-Islamic remains incorporated into more recent houses: stone lintels on doors often bear pre-Islamic inscriptions indicating the 'quarry' from which they came. The original market place contains rudimentary porticos made with cylindrical columns. Despite several stone buildings, many displaying timber lattices of Turkish origin, the town is characterised by a mixed architecture with stone ground floors and projecting mud top floors. The corners of roof parapets are usually raised with a central triangle of soft contour. Windows have simple plaster borders occasionally of fanciful design. These buildings have strong affinities with Bani Hushaysh further east and the rural architecture around Sanᶜa'. *Top:* Stone walls and the Great Mosque *(foreground)* seen from the west. *Bottom:* The market.

239

*Top:* Characteristic houses, ᶜAmran. *Bottom:* West of ᶜAmran stone predominates, mud being used only for part or all of the top floor.

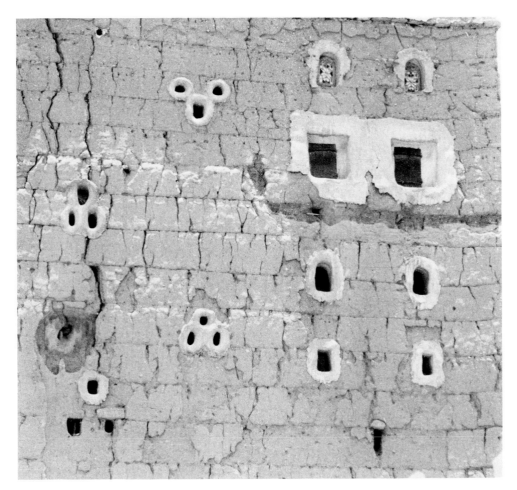

On the threshold of the Eastern Plateau is Bani Hushaysh, containing important pre-Islamic remnants and mud architecture co-existing with stone. Mud buildings display clay courses on the lower floors and *libn* brick on the top floors. The raised corners of the roofs may be underlined with white plaster; the fanlights are like those found in a wide area of mud architecture from ᶜAmran to Sanᶜa'. *Top:* Detail of mud wall. *Bottom:* Building with typical features.

South-east of Bani Hushaysh are three isolated regions — Sinhan, Khawlan and al-Hada' — the people of which are known for their war-like spirit. Sinhan contains a number of stone settlements similar in style to the Khamir-Dhi Bin area to the north, but more characteristic are its tall mud houses, as in Khawlan, with a strongly fortified aspect. The typical projecting cornice is locally explained as both a decorative feature and a way of diverting rain from the walls. *Zabur* is used for the ground floors and *libn* for the upper storeys, though the stone foundation may be high enough to sometimes include the ground floor. *Below:* Al-Hajlah, Khawlan.

*(Opposite) Top:* Settlement gate, an-Najda'i, Khawlan. *Bottom:* Al-Jihana, the most important market town between San⸵a' and Ma'rib, in Khawlan.

*Top Right:* Isolated rural house near al-Jihana, Khawlan. *Centre Left:* Mud frieze and ventilation holes, al-Jihana. *Bottom:* Rural compound near al-Jihana. Note *(on the right)* the projecting top floor built in *libn*, clearly the living quarters.

On the south-east fringe of the Great Arabian Desert are Ma'rib and Harib. Ma'rib was heavily bombed in the Civil War and is now largely in ruins. Intact buildings are constructed in mud over stone foundations pillaged from monuments. The style of Harib with its one-and multi-storey buildings, quadrangular windows and red ochre decoration, combines architectural elements from the Eastern Plateau with decorative elements from

the south-eastern mountains. *Centre and Bottom Right:* Facade and bathroom of Harib houses. *Top Left:* Ma'rib. *Bottom Left:* Low house, Harib.

The south-east extends from the fringes of the desert to the desolate mountains between Radaᶜ and al-Bayda', an area where nomads settled in small low settlements or quadrangular schist towers. The influence of these towers is seen in larger settlements, including the provincial capital - al-Bayda'. In this region stone and mud architecture exists side-by-side, displaying a similar outline and similar devices such as openings, but with other separate features. Combinations occur, with stone being used for the ground floors and mud for the upper part of the building. Despite a severe appearance, especially in the schist stone towers, ornament is evident in the triangular inlaid designs made in stone and in the red ochre used around openings, along rooftops, in skirtings or covering small portions of upper floor walls facing the terraces in mud buildings. *Top Left:* Cluster of mud houses, al-Zahir. *Centre Left:* Chequered decoration of door tympanum, an-Ghawl. *Bottom:* Al-Hawyin. The stocky polygonal minarets *(right side)* are exclusive to this area.

*(Opposite)* Parallel architectures, as-Sawma'ah. Note the supplementary square openings above the main windows, which provide additional ventilation and light.

*Top:* As-Sawma'ah. These decorations made in thick plaster on stone walls are most popular in this small village and other settlements further north. *Bottom:* Houses facing the older core of the settlement, al-Ajradi (see p. 29). The one-storey house on the right is in the latest fashion in the region of al-Bayda', with joints geometrically underlined in white and an arched plaster surface, sometimes coloured with enamel paint around the top square windows.

In al-Bayda', the capital, mud houses appear together with embellished stone houses, especially in older constructions. More recent houses favour a plainer form in which stone dominates, mud being often restricted to the top floor. The sharp raised corners, so characteristic of provincial architecture, here give place to straight roof lines, although in some buildings the roof is topped by a crown of scallop shapes. Square openings above the main windows become large rectangles with the size of the base doubled. In older constructions windows have latticed shutters of quality workmanship, now be-

ing replaced by iron burglar bars. Post-Revolution buildings maintain the same overall structure and height but display similar facade treatment to the al-Ajradi example opposite. *Top:* Al-Bayda', dominated by a fortress on the hilltop. Note the domed tombs in the cemetery *(foreground). Centre:* View from house rooftop. This house is surveyed on page 252.

*Top Right and Left:* The new and the old architectural styles. *Bottom:* Mud buildings.

*(Opposite) Top Right and Left:* Decorated stone house of the old style; interior of house. *Bottom:* Facade of mud house. Note windows and drainage pipes.

*Below:* Detail of terrace parapet. *Top Left:* Interior view of windows. *Centre Right:* Detail of *mafraj* section. Mattresses here are raised 40-50 cm. either by additional mattresses or by a masonry bench. *Bottom Right: Dihliz. Centre and Bottom Left:* Floor plans.

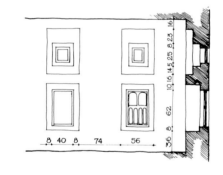

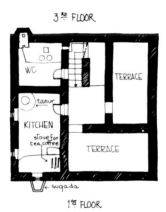

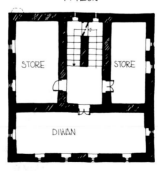

2<sup>ND</sup> FLOOR

VACANT

FATHER'S ROOM

liquid waste drain

cradle

masfa

bed

bed

GRANDFATHER'S ROOM (SITTING, SLEEPING)

3<sup>RD</sup> FLOOR

WC

TERRACE

tanur

KITCHEN

stove for tea, coffee

TERRACE

suqada

HATAB (WOOD STORE)

KIRS

COWS

GROUND FLOOR

ta'hun

DIHLIS (ENTRANCE) HALL

SHEEP

CHICKEN

HAWSH (YARD)

1<sup>ST</sup> FLOOR

STORE

STORE

DIWAN

50   300
0  100   cm

Halfway between al-Bayda' and Rada$^c$, settlements are of one- or two-storey buildings, occasionally with a protective tower. Construction is in stone with a mud surface. *Top:* Khawah. *Centre:* The plains before Rada$^c$. *Bottom Right:* Sheikh's house, Bayt al-Jabri — a blend of styles, in shape and material this stone building belongs to a more southerly style; the windows however are typical of Rada$^c$.

# 8. URBAN SYNTHESES

Although mud and stone are often combined in a construction with homogeneous effect, each material is usually treated in a distinctive way. Thus, all the elements that compose the style of stone lower floors will express the language of stone architecture and all the elements that compose the style of mud top floors express the language of mud architecture. There are a few instances when the general effect is such that, at first sight, it is difficult to determine which material determines the style of the construction. However, examples of such syntheses exist, usually in an urban context which unifies the varied architectural forms it contains. The cases presented next are examples of different urban centres: Radaͨ, a small local capital; Dhamar, a larger regional capital; and Sanͨa', the present capital of the Yemen Arab Republic. Radaͨ illustrates a synthesis of materials — mud and brick; Dhamar exemplifies a synthesis of materials — mud, brick and stone — and a synthesis of urban space on a wider scale in which possible combinations of materials define characteristic areas of the town; in Sanͨa, the co-existence of various building materials defines each element in the townscape and these together determine the character of the city.

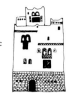

Rada<sup>c</sup>, the most important town in the southern half of the Eastern Plateau, contains some remarkable examples of 12th century Ayyubid religious architecture. The town lies on a flat wide plain, at the foot of a high rocky outcrop where its fort-citadel is strategically located. Its main western gate still stands, together with sections of stone wall. Most of the architecture is of mud, although stone may be used for the ground floor, and there are some, usually governmental, buildings wholly of stone and brick in adapted styles.

Although the town's public spaces are somewhat neglected, the external aspects of buildings show concern for their outside appearance. The quality of mud construction is refined, including brickwork in the mud walls both as a structural element for the arches of openings and for decorative purposes. Most window fanlights are made by double or triple arches, each containing the largest possible single pane of alabaster. The double arch with alabaster above the windows and the fusion of mud and brick in construction and ornamentation are the most original elements of Rada<sup>c</sup> architecture. *Below:* Rada<sup>c</sup> — a general view.

Interiors are characterised by an intimacy largely created by the exclusive use of alabaster in fanlights, occasionally punctuated by small openings with coloured glass fretwork *(takhrim). Top:* Interior of 4th floor *mandar. Right:* Plans and section of the same house.

*(Opposite)* Brick decorations are set in mud walls in friezes and around openings. The corners of the bricks are cut, a simple device characteristic of this region. The calligraphic 'potential' of brick ornamentation is widely exploited here in Koranic inscriptions on facades or the tops of walls.

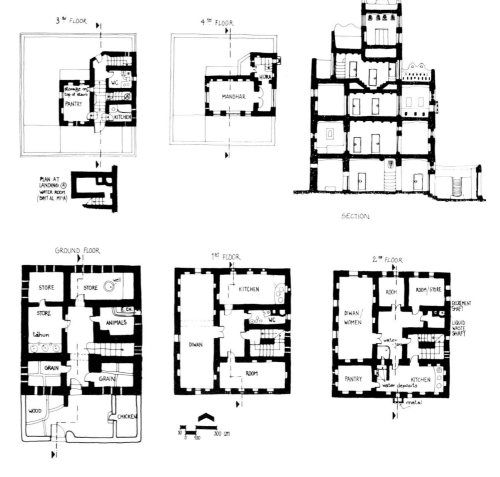

*Centre Right:* In contrast with its buildings, the streets of Rada<sup>c</sup> are a neutral undefined area where waste is thrown. *Left:* Architectural synthesis.

The foundation of Dhamar, an important market town set in a fertile plain, goes back to *himyaritic* times. Except for the old Jewish neighbourhood, the town is unwalled, being protected by fortresses in the surrounding hills. The architecture of Dhamar combines mud, brick and stone in ways that define the various neighbourhoods. Each material has a specific function: brick inlays decorate stone or mud walls, and stone arches are structural elements in mud or brick walls. Alabaster is common for fanlights in multiple openings or in single panes; *takhrim* occur in similar types of frame. The use of alternating bands of dark and light lava-stone is widespread, and especially so in modern stone architecture in the region. *Bottom Right:* Old stone building with alternating black and white bands and decorative brick insets. Note the abundance of wooden distribution joists. *Bottom Left:* Synthesis of forms and materials in one building.

*Top Left:* The market of Dhamar, with its paved squares, streets and alleys, is exceptional. *Bottom:* Walls of the old and large Jewish neighbourhood. Sanᶜa' is the only other large town with a confined Jewish neighbourhood, called Qa' al-Yahud ('the Jews' quarter'). The houses are all of mud, and in all respects similar to other mud houses in the town except for the top courtyard.

*(Opposite) Centre Left and Bottom:* Old mud house of noble family in the town centre, with top court and lightwells for the lower hallways. Note the superimposed rounds for the fanlights characteristic of stone and/or brick buildings. *Top: Mandar* of top floor and roof terraces. Note the chimney — a cooking-oil can with the sides opened out. *Centre Right:* Mud stair from entrance hall *(dihliz)* to grinding mills *(tahun).*

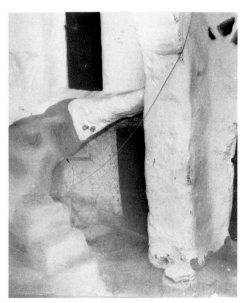

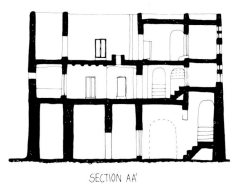

SECTION AA'

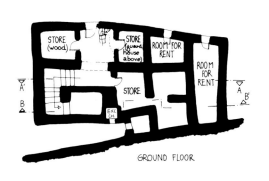

GROUND FLOOR

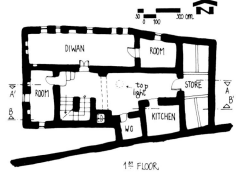

1ˢᵀ FLOOR

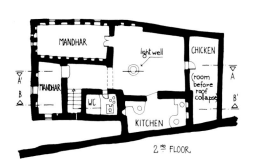

2ᴺᴰ FLOOR

In Dhamar different materials are often combined in the same wall. *Top:* A mud building with brick decoration and, on a brick frame, a large window with multiple alabaster panes. *Bottom:* A large building with similar features. Note the double rounds for the fanlights, set in brick in a stone arch. *Centre:* Plans of upper floors of a stone and brick house with top court and lightwells.

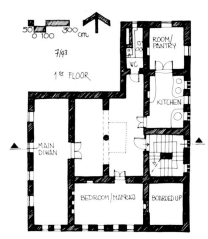

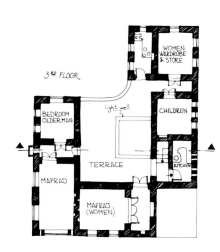

*Top Right:* Large twin houses with brick top floor and connecting bridge. Note the parapet made of blind arches, a common feature of 'grand' buildings (*opposite* is another example), and *(in the foreground)* more recently-built shops. *Bottom:* Recent buildings and shop door. The post-Revolution architecture of Dhamar uses stone; bands of black and white lava stone and triangular inlays are the main decorative features. Simple inset stone friezes also occur. The appearance of these buildings is severe, very different from the imaginative variety of even the recent past. Yet in terms of stone finishing and decorative patterns, contemporary architecture in Dhamar is more successful than in most other centres of stone architecture (including Sanᶜa') that are still experiencing the crisis provoked by the sudden exposure to new materials and forms of construction.

# 8. URBAN SYNTHESES

(Sanᶜa') *is the former capital of the country of al-Yaman, a large and well constructed city, built with bricks and plaster, with many trees and fruits and with a temperate climate and good weather . . . The whole city of Sanᶜa' is paved and when the rain falls it washes and cleans all its streets. The cathedral mosque of Sanᶜa' is one of the finest of mosques and contains the grave of one of the prophets (peace be upon them).* (The travels of Ibn Battuta).

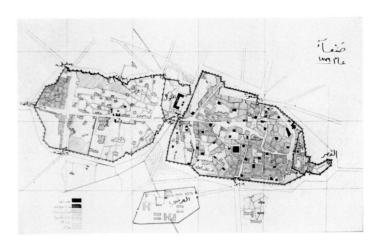

The city of Sanᶜa' is situated in the geographic centre of Yemen, in the middle of a vast plateau 2,500 m. high at the foot of Jabal Nuqum, on the top of which a military garrison occupies a stronghold dating from pre-Islamic times. Most houses are a combination of stone (for the lower floors) and brick (for the top floors), while mud constructions are found in the poorer areas and in rural settlements around the town. Until the Civil War the city was contained within two walled parts separated by a cemetery and large gardens containing one of the main gates. Egyptian initiative during the Civil War led to the opening of a modern centre — an avenue with double carriageway, shops and apartment buildings — over the cemetery and the gardens. The city has grown rapidly since 1968, doubling in size every four years and engulfing the surrounding villages. This brief survey will describe three main areas — the *madina*, the oldest part inside the easternmost wall, Bi'r al-ᶜAzab, a suburb once confined by the walls on the western half, and west of this the Qa' al-Yahud, the Jewish neighbourhood. Developments now taking place will also be noted. *Top:* Sanᶜa' in 1880, 1962 and 1964. The boundaries re-

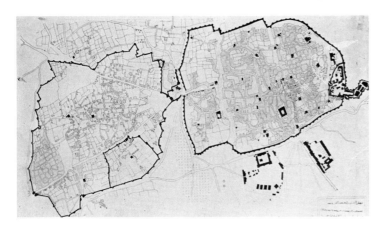

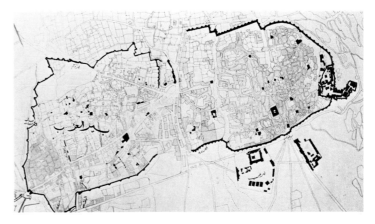

mained unchanged until the walls were broken at the junction of the two main areas — the *madina (east, on the right)* and the suburban gardens and buildings *(west, on the left)*. At the most eastern point of the *madina* is an enclosed fortification which was probably the old citadel. The dense settlement on the far left was the Jewish area. Most of the *madina* houses are concentrated on the eastern bank of a seasonal water course, the *sayla;* the area between the *sayla* and the western wall contains orchards, some semi-surburban houses, a market (connected to the main gate) and two mosques. *Bottom:* Sanᶜa' in 1976 seen from a roof in the *madina*.

The *madina* contains the most complete examples of Yemeni urban architecture including innumerable mosques, the most remarkable of which were built or renovated under the Turks. One exception is the Great Mosque, one of the oldest in Yemen, which is in part pre-Islamic and has been frequently enlarged and restored. Adjoining the Great Mosque is Suq al-Milh, a complex market organised according to professional sectors, with an elaborate system of merchants' guilds and market leaders (Sheikhs of the Suqs). *Below:* Suq al-Milh. *Bottom Left:* A night watchmen's guardhouse.

*(Opposite) Top:* Looking south from the *madina* to the outlying villages. Six years later San<sup>c</sup>a' spread all the way to the last village. *Bottom:* Walls of the *madina*.

The houses rise from amidst large gardens not always visible from the facade-lined streets. Gardens and orchards are traditionally fertilised by the ashes of sanitary waste, burnt as fuel for the hot bathhouses. These gardens, tended by vegetable growers *(qashshamun)*, produce a range of fresh vegetables for the city market. *Below:* Gardens inside the city.

The streets, no longer paved as in the days of Ibn Battuta, are frequently bridged over and enlivened by a great variety of facade ornamentation. At night, especially during Ramadan when everybody is up late, *takhrim* cast their coloured lights onto the dark streets with magical effect. *This page:* Bridges connecting houses.

*(Overleaf)* Stone and brick facades. Plaster designs are applied directly onto the wall or over the face of brick inlays.

# 8. URBAN SYNTHESES

A fine example of a *madina* house, with ground floor and mezzanine serving agricultural needs (though there are no animals in the house, fruit and grain are still stored here) and elaborately treated living quarters. *Bottom Left:* General view. *Right Side:* Sections A-B (note the shaft leading from the ground-floor well to the top-floor kitchen) and C-D.

*(Opposite) Top: Dihliz* and floor plans. *Bottom Left:* Well at entrance yard. *Centre Right:* Masonry storage bins for fruit and grain in mezzanine *(tabaqa al-hab)*. *Bottom Right: Tahun.*

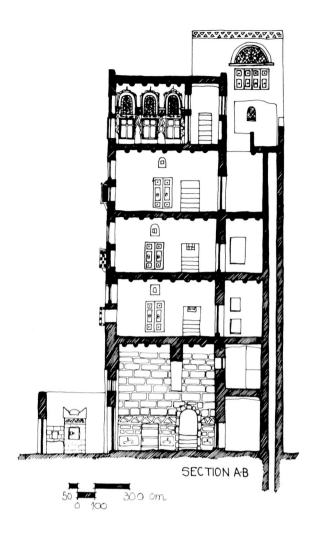

SECTION A-B

50 | 300 cm
0 100

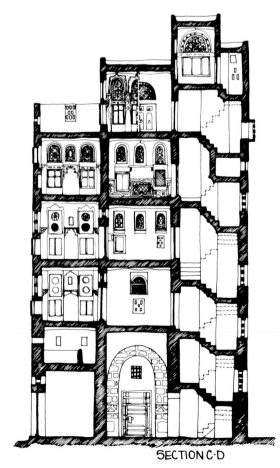

SECTION C-D

272

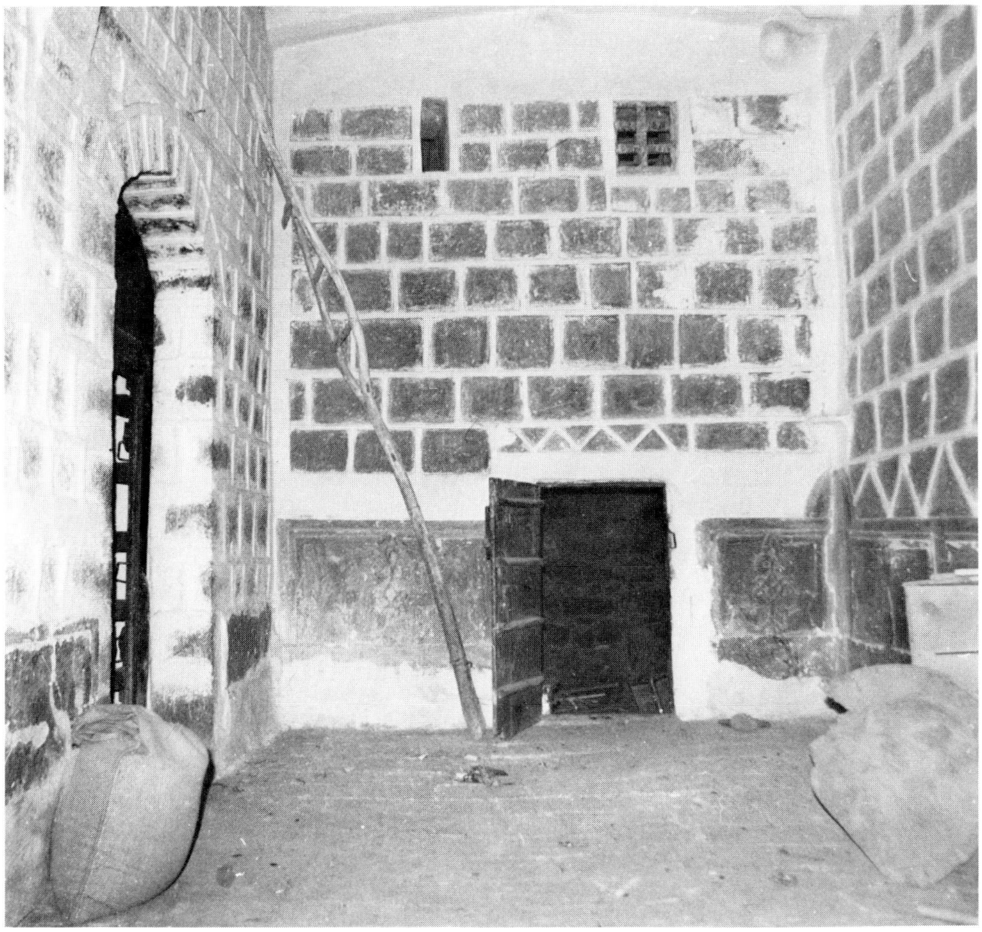

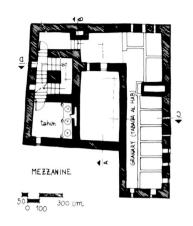

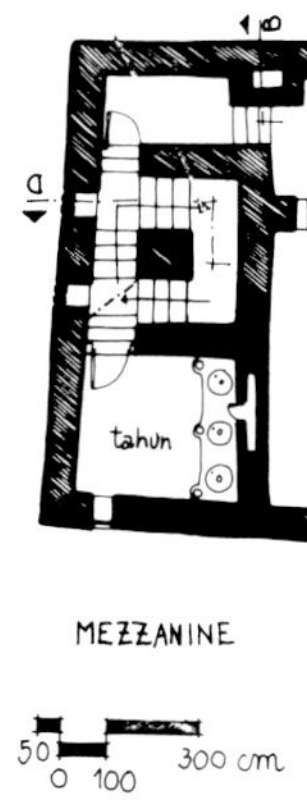
tahun
GRANARY (TABAQA AL HAB)
MEZZANINE
50 0 100 300 cm

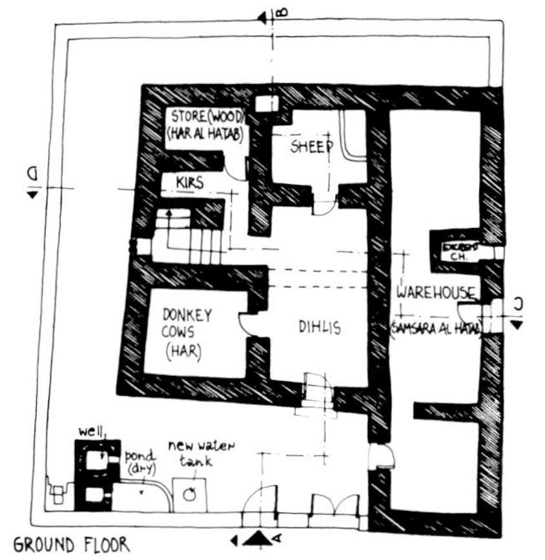
STORE (WOOD) (HAR AL HATAB)
SHEEP
KIRS
DONKEY COWS (HAR)
DIHLIS
WAREHOUSE
SAMSARA AL HATAB
well
pond (dry)
new water tank
GROUND FLOOR

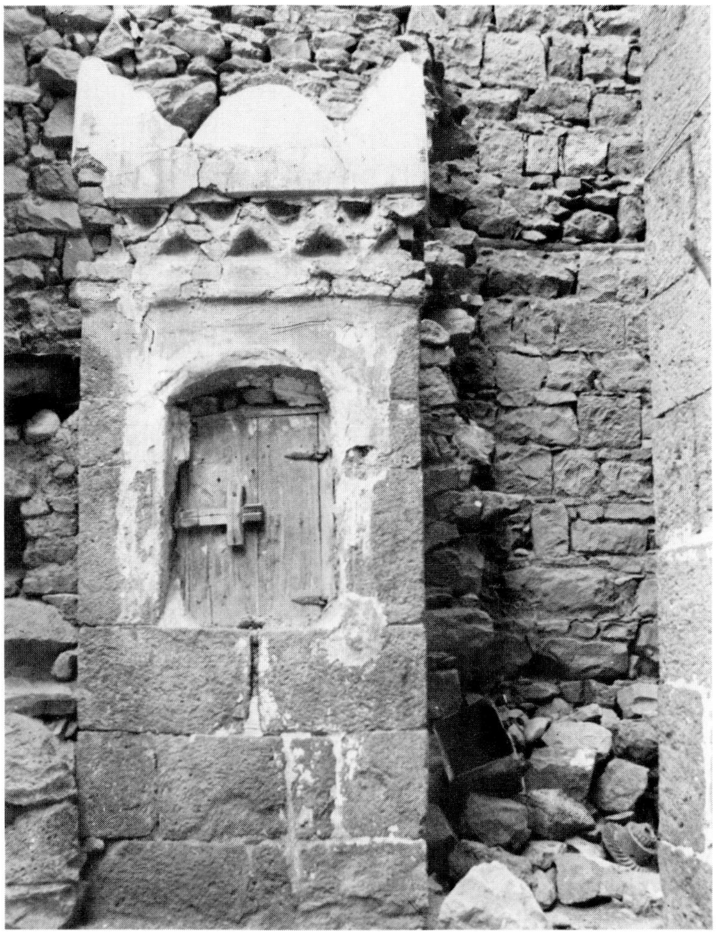

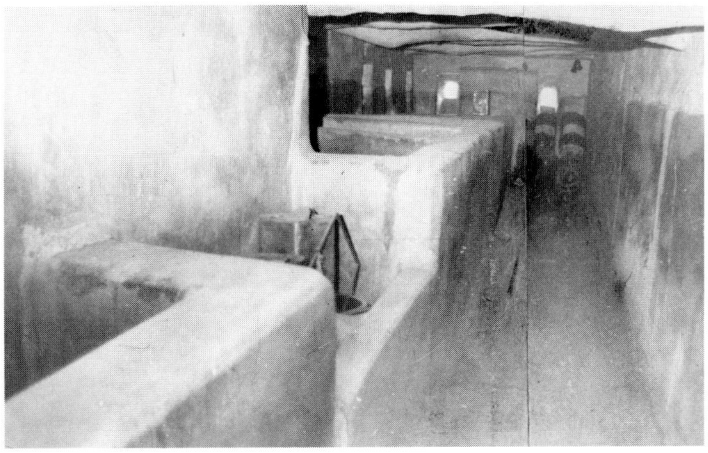

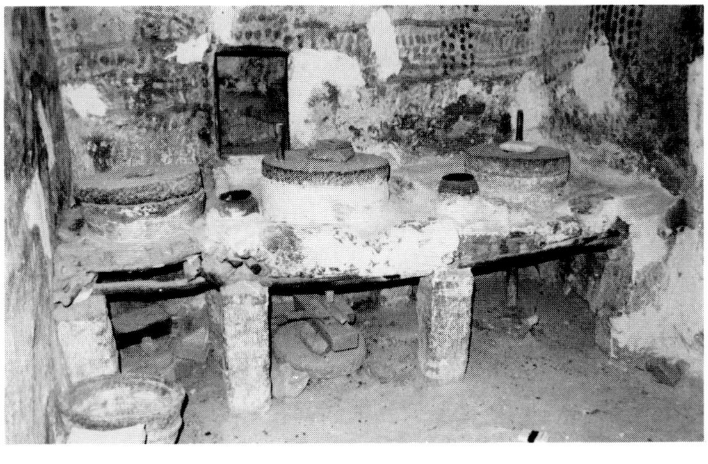

In this large house, as elsewhere, function varies according to season: people use the warmer rooms in winter and the cooler ones in summer. *Below:* Floor plans and great *diwan* on second floor *(al-mandar al-wusta).*

*(Opposite) Top, from Left to Right:* Stair seen from hallway, *(hijra),* 4th floor; door of great *mafraj,* 4th floor; roof terrace, contiguous to 5th floor. *Centre:* Floor plans. *Bottom Left:* Hallway *(sa'la),* 3rd floor. Note skirtings made with waterproofed *nura* (lime plaster rubbed with a mixture of cow grease and alabaster powder). *Bottom Right:* Terrace on top of kitchen, 4th floor, with masonry receptacle for rain water ducted from upper roof terraces.

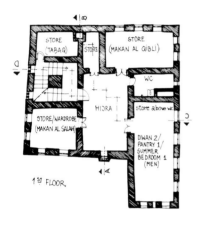

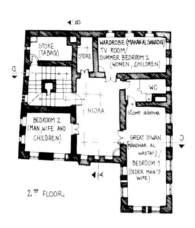

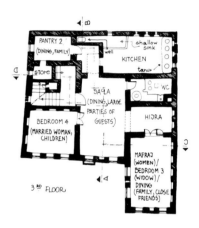

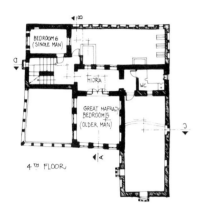

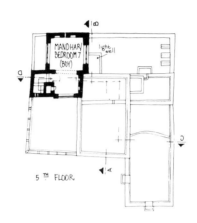

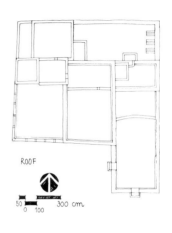

4 TH FLOOR

5 TH FLOOR

ROOF

50  300 cm
0  100

# 8. URBAN SYNTHESES

The houses in Bi'r al-ʿAzab are similar in plan to the *madina,* though with fewer storeys and simpler volumes. Decorative emphasis is given to friezes and *takhrim* designs made in arches. There are no superimposed rounds or elaborate plaster designs and brick inlays so common in the *madina.* The composition of the facade is symmetrical with a regular pattern of wide and narrow windows. There is often a ground floor receiving/sitting room (*mafraj*) with an arched porch abutting a patio with a pond and continuing to the gardens. This is also a feature of summer leisure houses in surburban villages and is similar to the ground-floor *diwans* in coastal Turkish houses. *Centre Left and Bottom:* Typical ornamentation. Note the Turkish influence in timber awnings and latticed windows. *Top and Centre Right:* Sketch of building with ground-floor *mafraj* in al-Rawda; porch, pond and patio fence of ground floor *mafraj* in Bab al-Sabah.

*(Opposite) Top:* Bi'r al-ʿAzab. *Bottom Right and Left:* Ground floor plan and view of two houses with ground-floor *mafraj.*

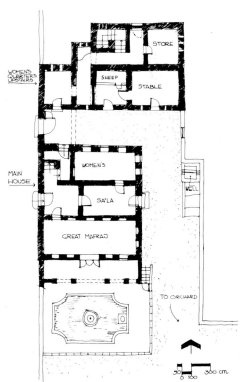

*(Opposite)* Smaller houses with proportional fanlights: the chamber equals 1.5 times the embrasure. *Top:* The timber latticed windows are of Jewish origin. Note the plaster gratings, one of the few examples still standing. *Bottom:* Behind is the Presidential Palace built for the last Imams, one of a few houses totally built in stone.

*Centre: Mafraj* on top floor and stairway window of two-storey house belonging to a family of Turkish descent. The measured drawing shows the wall facing west and the garden. *Bottom:* Bi'r al-ᶜAzab has suffered from the construction of a new commercial thoroughfare between the zone separating this quarter from the *madina* and its western limit; prime areas have been extensively demolished and gardens chaotically filled in by new constructions.

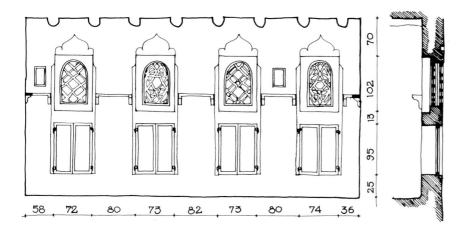

Mud buildings house the poorer classes and rural immigrants from the country-side. Thus, on the fringes of Bi'r al-ᶜAzab there are provincial elements in the architecture. *Top:* Mud house with brick elements. The plastering around the openings is a northern fashion from the region of Saᶜda. *Bottom:* A row of identical mud houses built for ex-soldiers with structural and decorative elements in plastered white brick.

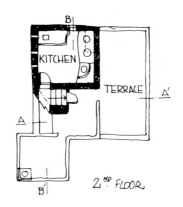

2<sup>ND</sup> FLOOR

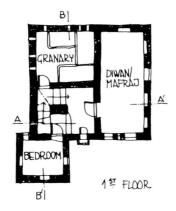

1<sup>ST</sup> FLOOR

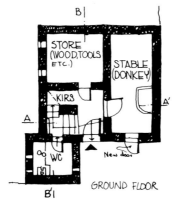

GROUND FLOOR

The outside of this house belies the quality of its interior. Built in the Jewish quarter, though not a Jewish house, its small rooms are distributed in half-floors along the stair landings. *Top:* Exterior view and *tannur* of kitchen (recently re-plastered). *Centre and Bottom: Mafraj,* floor plans and section.

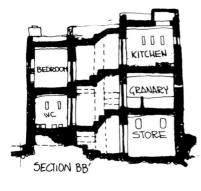

SECTION BB'

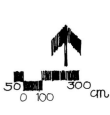

281

# 8. URBAN SYNTHESES

Al-Qa', the Jewish quarter until 1948, is on the western extreme of Bi'r al-ʿAzab, formerly separated by a wall. The architecture is of mud, or mud and brick, though some brick houses existed for important community members. Houses here were subject to special laws concerning the height of buildings (no more than two normal storeys) and their aspect, which could not be ostentatious. Thus the height of the rooms was lowered so that small rooms or alcoves could exist in half-floors. These rooms are articulated around a central top court, the most distinctive feature of Jewish architecture in Sanʿa', which shows strong links with top-court houses found throughout the country. Houses often contained secret chambers and exits connecting adjacent buildings not only to protect goods but also to allow rapid evacuation during raids and in times of persecution. Now the neighbourhood is changing: the Jews have left the country, the small rooms and alcoves are being demolished to make loftier spaces, and entire houses are being demolished. *Below:* A street today.

*(Opposite) Top Left:* Mud wall. *Top Right:* Carved wooden door of market stall. *Bottom:* House with top court.

## 8. URBAN SYNTHESES

Fanlights are usually in alabaster although *takhrim* also exist with minute designs or framing a central alabaster pane. The most common fanlight shapes are arches and superimposed squares with round alabaster panes. These alabaster panes are now being replaced by glass or *takhrim* of mediocre design, as elsewhere in the country. *Top Right:* Alabaster fanlights in arches and rectangles. *Centre Left:* Alabaster fanlights with a coloured glass frame. *Bottom: Takhrim* of typical Jewish design.

Detail of facade with typically Jewish styled lattice casement.

SECTION

*Top and Bottom Right:* Section and facade of house surveyed opposite. *Top Left:* A room formerly used for the feast of the tabernacles *(Sukkah).* The ceiling hole was covered from the roof with easily removable material so that it could be opened to the sky once a year for the Jewish harvest feast of Thanksgiving. *Bottom Left:* Detail of large receiving room of another house showing door to a raised alcove.

*(Opposite)* Floor plans, aspects of court and stair to court of house.

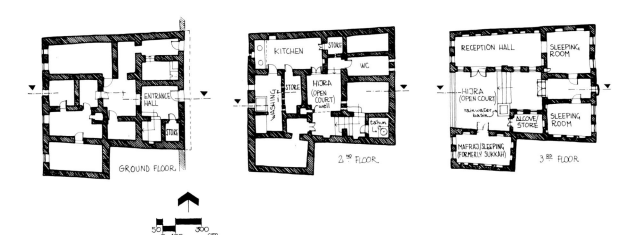

ENTRANCE HALL · STORE · GROUND FLOOR

KITCHEN · STORE · STORE · WC · WASHING · STORE · HIJRA (OPEN COURT) well · tahun · 2ⁿᵈ FLOOR

RECEPTION HALL · SLEEPING ROOM · HIJRA (OPEN COURT) · rain water basin · ALCOVE/STORE · SLEEPING ROOM · MAFRAJ/SLEEPING (FORMERLY SUKKAH) · 3ᴿᴰ FLOOR

50 0 100 300 cm

New Sanⁿa' begins at the new 'main street' and its branches. The building forms introduced here are the same as in Taⁿizz and al-Hudayda — concrete apartment buildings with showy colours and standard patterns. In Sanⁿa', however, stone rapidly became the prestige material for new buildings, following a trend in palace construction adopted by the last Imams. Now stone construction incorporates reinforced concrete walls and roof slabs with load bearing walls with concrete frames. The results are a pastiche of traditional architecture. Potentially more interesting is the work of builders experimenting with techniques and materials adapted from their local traditions. *Top Left: Mafraj* of 'villa'. *Bottom Right:* Shariⁿ ⁿAbd al-Mughniy, the main modern street. *Bottom Left:* A building displaying three successive forms of construction: stone, concrete and brick.

*(Opposite)* The Government Guest House, planned by a foreign architect and flamboyantly executed by the son of a master mason. *Centre:* Foreign versions of traditional architecture: Ministry of Justice *(Left)*; University *(Right)*. *Bottom Left:* New neighbourhoods, hurriedly built in stone, have a drab look. *Bottom Right:* Stone ground-floor with concrete top.

Many of the small mud villages around Sanᶜa' include round mud towers topped by square rooms. Two of these villages, ar-Rawda and Wadi Dahr, have long been areas where the wealthy kept summer houses. Al-Rawda has its own type of surburban brick architecture, in many respects similar to that of Bi'r al-ᶜAzab. Wadi Dahr, set in a fertile valley surrounded by steep cliffs, is a scenic spot where people often go to chew qat. Its mud and brick architecture reflects the social differences between local farmers and urban dwellers. Wadi Dahr contains an architectural gem, the Dar al-Hajar (house of rock), the summer house of a former Imam, set on a rocky outcrop (illustrated on p. 1). *Centre:* Qariya al-Djaj on the northern outskirts of Sanᶜa'. *Bottom:* Ar-Rawda.

*(Opposite) Top:* The orchards of Wadi Dahr seen from the cliffs. *Bottom:* Plans and *diwan* of a mud house.

*(Overleaf)* Street in al-Qa', Sanᶜa'.

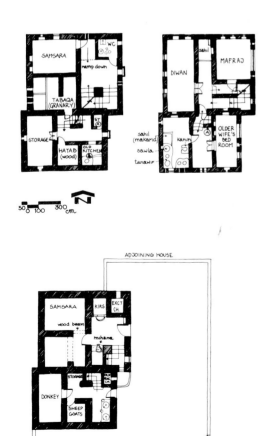

# GLOSSARY OF TECHNICAL TERMS

| | |
|---|---|
| amil | provincial government representative (administrative post with no religious authority attached to it, cf. Hakim, *qadi* qqv.) |
| aqd (pl. *uqud*) | decorative fanlight making up the upper part of a window |
| ballat | layer of tiles |
| ballu'a | cesspool digger |
| barud | shaded area outside a house |
| basut | joist |
| bayt | house, also designates a patronymic lineage, as well as a group of houses named after the original family who were settled in them |
| bint al-wusuda | soft cushion, pillow |
| biyya' | tradesman |
| dayma | guardshouse |
| dharwa | covered area of a coastal house |
| dihliz | entrance hall to a tower house |
| diwan | reception room |
| dubr | angle stone |
| farsh | floor, mattresses |
| funduq | inn |
| galfa | inner wall stone |
| hajar wajh | facade, stone |
| hakim | judge |
| hammam | bath |
| hijra | ante-chamber |
| himyari | natural or man-made caves used as stables, storage space or shelter |
| hukuma | government building |
| jami' | mosque |
| jurn | communal grain threshing floor |
| juss | gypsum plaster work |
| kanun | small stove |
| kharja | roof terrace of a coastal house |
| kunna | ornamental board over a window |
| libn | sun-dried mud blocks |
| mada'a | water pipe |
| madfan | underground grain storage pit |
| madqa | arm-rest |
| mafraj | belvedere |
| mafraj al-istiqbal | reception room |
| mafraj al majnu'a | gathering room |
| mafrasha | rug |
| maghfara | niche |
| majil | open cistern to collect rain or run-off water |
| malaj | gypsum or mud ceiling surfacing tiles |
| manzar | main room (literally "with a view") |
| mardam | sill stone |
| masfa | ablution room |
| mat'hana | grinding mill |
| mawfar | outdoor mud store or oven |

| | |
|---|---|
| mihrab | prayer niche in a mosque |
| mu'allim | master |
| muqawwil | contractor |
| muqassis | stone cutter |
| muwaqqus | mason |
| nawb | watchtower |
| nura | lime plaster |
| qadi | judge |
| qahira | fort |
| qamariya | decorative piece of arched alabaster on a fanlight |
| qat | intoxicating herb chewed in Yemen |
| qdad | mixture of plaster, coal and alabaster |
| qishr | peel, brewed as a drink |
| qutb | stone newel |
| rassas | mason |
| rawshan | balcony |
| sabil | ablution pool in a mosque |
| sahil | washing trough |
| sala | hallway |
| samsarah | warehouse |
| saqf | room, also designates mountain stone shelters |
| sfaf | plaster shelves |
| shaqi | day labourer |
| shahada | raised stones dedicated to Allah on the corners of mosque roofs |
| shamsiya | top floor courtyard in a house |
| shaqus | wall ventilation slits |
| shubbak | window, also the observation casement in a watch tower and a cooling box in a house |
| sunduq | niche |
| suq | market |
| tabaqat al abb | grain storage level in a house |
| tahein | grinding mill |
| takhrim | plaster and glass fretwork |
| talmidh | pupil |
| tannur | mud oven |
| thana | mason |
| ujra | wage |
| 'ulama | learned man (sing. *'alim*) |
| uqud | fanlights |
| usta | master mason |
| wadi | fertile valley with watercourse |
| wajl | stone facade |
| wali | holy, revered man |
| wasada | hard cushions to support the back |
| yajur | baked bricks |
| zabur | clay courses |
| zakat | tax |

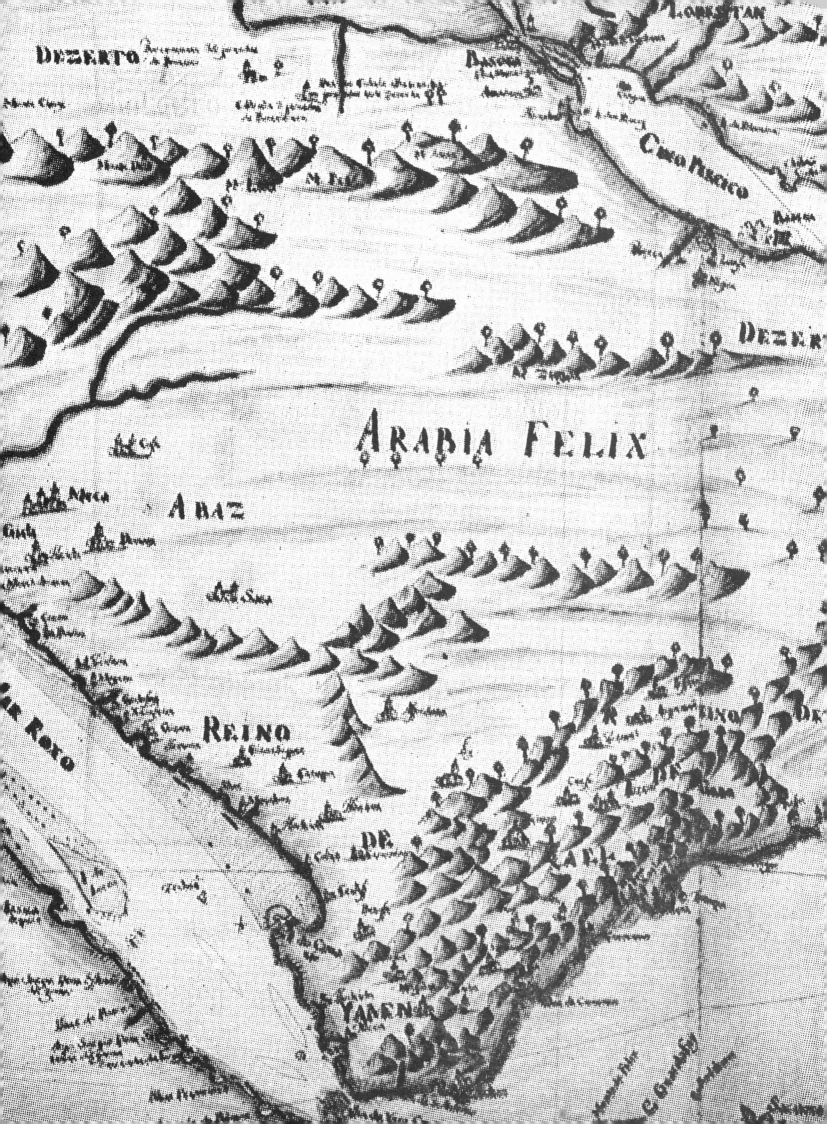